he Pocket Guide to Opera

The Pocket Guide to Opera

Anna Selby

REMEMBER WHEN

First published in Great Britain in 2011 by
REMEMBER WHEN
an imprint of
Pen & Sword Books Ltd
47 Church Street
Barnsley
South Yorkshire
S70 2AS

ISBN 978 1 84468 086 3

A CIP catalogue record for this book is
available from the British Library.

Printed and bound by CPI Antony Rowe, Chippenham and Eastbourne

Pen & Sword Books Ltd incorporates the imprints of
Pen & Sword Aviation, Pen & Sword Maritime, Pen & Sword Military,
Wharncliffe Local History, Pen & Sword Select, Pen & Sword Military Classics,
Leo Cooper, Remember When, Seaforth Publishing and Frontline Publishing

For a complete list of Pen & Sword titles please contact
PEN & SWORD BOOKS LIMITED
47 Church Street, Barnsley, South Yorkshire, S70 2AS, England
E-mail: enquiries@pen-and-sword.co.uk
Website: www.pen-and-sword.co.uk

CONTENTS

FOREWORD

Opera has been with us for centuries and has worn many guises. From its earliest beginnings in court masques and mystery plays to its mass appeal in nineteenth-century Italy to the rather elitist image it acquired in the twentieth, it keeps on changing – or at least our attitude towards it does. Nowadays, you are just as likely to come across opera as an opener to the World Cup or on a TV advert as you are in an opera house. So, as more and more people hear at least snippets of the great operas, it is no surprise that there is a new generation of opera-goers who come to it fresh and want to know more. This book is designed to help them find their way with a guide to the top fifty operas and an introduction to the greatest composers, singers, librettists and conductors who have conjured magic over the centuries. Open your mind and your heart – and enjoy.

Anna Selby

TIME CHART

1600   The 'Camerata', a group of intellectual aristocrats meeting in Florence, including Count Giovanni Bardi di Vernio, Jacopo Corsi, Vincenzo Galilei (father of the astronomer), Emilio de' Cavalieri and Jacopo Peri, vowed to create the combining of words and music so that the drama was expressed through the music as it was, they believed, in the ancient Greek theatre.

1607   *Orfeo*, Monteverdi, was the first opera to draw on the Camerata's theories and make them work musically and dramatically.

1637   Opening of first public opera house in Venice. Another fifteen were built by the end of the century.

1658   Birth of Purcell.

1669   Establishment of the Opéra (Académie Royale de Musique) in Paris.

1671   Pierre Perrin and Robert Cambert write the first French opera, *Pomone*.

1673   Lully sets the pattern for French opera for the next hundred years with *Cadmus et Hermione*, with a strong emphasis on recitative, with music following poetry and stories from myth and the chivalric tradition.

1685   Birth of Handel.

1689   Purcell's *Dido and Aeneas* premiered in London.

1695   Death of Purcell.

1711   Handel's first opera, *Rinaldo*, premiered at the Haymarket, London, and soon thereafter in Dublin, Hamburg and Naples.

1718   Handel's only opera written in English premiered, *Acis and Galatea*, with words by John Gay.

1728   John Gay's ballad opera *The Beggar's Opera* premiered in Lincoln's Inn Fields, London.

1756   Birth of Mozart.

1759	Death of Handel.
1762	First performance of Gluck's *Orfeo ed Euridice* in Vienna, libretto by Ranieri da Calzabigi, and the first 'reform' opera, designed to restore true dramatic expression after a period of florid virtuosity.
1770	Birth of Beethoven.
1781	First performance of Mozart's *opera seria*, *Idomeneo*, in Munich – his first major adult opera and one of the last to feature a starring *castrato*.
1786	First performance in Vienna of Mozart's *The Marriage of Figaro* and the beginning of his collaboration with librettist Lorenzo da Ponte.
1791	Death of Mozart.
	Birth of Meyerbeer.
1792	Birth of Rossini.
1797	Birth of Donizetti.
1803	Birth of Berlioz.
1805	First performance of Beethoven's *Fidelio* in Vienna.
1813	Birth of Wagner.
	Birth of Verdi.
1816	First performance of *The Barber of Seville* by Rossini in Rome.
1818	Birth of Gounod.
1821	First performance of von Weber's *Der Freischütz* in Berlin.
1825	Birth of Johann Strauss.
1827	Death of Beethoven.
1830	First performance of Donizetti's *Anna Bolena* in Milan.
1831	First performance of Bellini's *La Sonnambula* in Milan.
	First performance of Bellini's *Norma* in Milan.
1835	First performance of Donizetti's *Lucia di Lammermoor* in Naples.
1838	First performance of Berlioz' *Benvenuto Cellini* in Paris.
1840	Birth of Tchaikovsky.
1842	First performance of Glinka's *Ruslan and Lyudmila* in St Petersburg.
1843	First performance of Michael William Balfe's *The Bohemian Girl* in London.
	First performance of Donizetti's *Don Pasquale* in Paris.
1845	First performance of Wagner's *Tannhäuser* in Dresden.

1846	First performance of Berlioz's *La damnation de Faust* in Paris.
1847	First performance of Verdi's *Macbeth* in Florence.
1848	Death of Donizetti.
1850	First performance of Wagner's *Lohengrin* in Weimar.
1851	First performance of Verdi's *Rigoletto* in Venice.
1853	First performance of Verdi's *La Traviata* in Venice.
1858	First performance of Offenbach's *Orpheus in the Underworld* in Paris.
	Birth of Puccini.
1859	First performance of Gounod's *Faust* in Paris.
	First performance of Verdi's *Un ballo in maschera* in Rome.
1863	First performance of Berlioz's *Les Troyens* in Paris.
	First performance of Bizet's *The Pearl Fishers* in Paris.
1864	Death of Meyerbeer.
	Birth of Richard Strauss.
1865	First performance of Wagner's *Tristan und Isolde* in Munich.
	First performance of Meyerbeer's *L'Africaine* in Paris.
1866	First performance of Smetana's *The Bartered Bride*.
1867	First performance of Verdi's *Don Carlos* in Paris.
1868	Death of Rossini.
1869	Death of Berlioz.
1871	First performance of Verdi's *Aida* in Milan.
1874	First performance of Gilbert and Sullivan's first collaboration, *Trial by Jury*, in London.
	First performance of Johann Strauss's *Die Fledermaus* (*The Bat*).
1875	First performance of Bizet's *Carmen* in Paris.
1876	First complete performance of Wagner's *Ring Cycle* in Bayreuth.
1877	First performance of Saint-Saëns' *Samson et Dalila* in Weimar.
1879	First performance of Tchaikovsky's *Eugene Onegin* in Moscow.
1881	First performance of Offenbach's *The Tales of Hoffman* in Paris.
1883	Death of Wagner.
	First performance of Delibes' *Lakmé* in Paris.
1884	First performance of Massenet's *Manon* in Paris.
1885	Birth of Alban Berg.
1886	First performance of Mussorgsky's *Khovanshchina* in St Petersburg.
1887	First performance of Verdi's *Otello* in Milan.

1890   First performance of Borodin's *Prince Igor* in St Petersburg.
       First performance of Tchaikovsky's *The Queen of Spades* in St Petersburg.
       First performance of Mascagni's *Cavalleria Rusticana* in Philadelphia.

1892   First performance of Alfredo Catalani's *La Wally* in Milan.
       First performance of Leoncavallo's *Pagliacci* in Milan.

1893   Death of Gounod.
       Death of Tchaikovsky.
       First performance of Puccini's *Manon Lescaut* in Turin.
       First performance of Verdi's *Falstaff* in Milan.

1896   First performance of Giordano's *Andrea Chenier* in Milan.
       First performance of *La Bohème* in Turin.
       First performance of Mussorgsky's *Boris Godunov* in its complete Rimsky-Korsakov revision in St Petersburg.

1900   First performance of Puccini's *Tosca* in Rome.

1901   Death of Verdi.
       First performance of Dvorák's *Rusalka* in Prague.

1902   First performance of Debussy's *Pelléas et Mélisande* in Paris.

1904   First performance of Puccini's *Madama Butterfly* in Milan.
       First performance of Janacek's *Jenufa* in Brno.

1905   First performance of Richard Strauss's *Salome* in Dresden.
       First performance of Lehár's *The Merry Widow* in Vienna.

1909   First performance of Richard Strauss's *Elektra* in Dresden.

1911   First performance of Richard Strauss's *Der Rosenkavalier* in Dresden.
       First performance of Ravel's *L'heure espagnole* in Paris.

1912   First performance of Richard Strauss's *Ariadne auf Naxos* in Stuttgart.

1913   First performance of Manuel de Falla's *La vida breve* in Nice.
       First performance of Fauré's *Penelope* in Monte Carlo.

1918   First performance of Bartók's *Duke Bluebeard's Castle* in Budapest.

1921   First performance of Prokofiev's *The Love of Three Oranges* in Chicago.
       First performance of Janacek's *Katya Kabanova* in Brno.

1924   First performance of Ralph Vaughan Williams' *Hugh the Drover* in London.

First performance of Janacek's *The Cunning Little Vixen* in Brno. Death of Puccini.

1925   First performance of Alban Berg's *Wozzeck* in Berlin.

1926   First performance of Puccini's *Turandot* in Milan.

1930   First performance of Kurt Weill's *Rise and Fall of the City of Mahagonny* in Berlin.

1933   First performance of Richard Strauss's *Arabella* in Vienna.

1934   First performance of Shostakovich's *Lady Macbeth of Mtsensk* in Moscow.

1935   Death of Alban Berg.
        First performance of Gershwin's *Porgy and Bess* in Boston.

1937   First performance of Berg's *Lulu* in Venice.

1945   First performance of Benjamin Britten's *Peter Grimes* in London.
        First performance of Prokofiev's *War and Peace* in Moscow.

1949   Death of Richard Strauss.

1951   First performance of Britten's *Billy Budd* in London.
        First performance of Stravinsky's *The Rake's Progress* in Venice.
        First television opera, Menotti's *Amahl and the Night Visitors*, produced for NBC Studios, New York.

1952   First performance of Hans Werner Henze's *Boulevard Solitude* in Hanover.

1954   First performance of Britten's *The Turn of the Screw* in Venice.
        First performance of William Walton's *Troilus and Cressida* in London.

1955   First performance of Michael Tippett's *The Midsummer Marriage* in London.

1957   First performance of Arnold Schoenberg's *Moses und Aron* in Zurich.

1968   First performance of Harrison Birtwistle's *Punch and Judy* at Aldeburgh.

1970   First performance of Michael Tippett's *The Knot Garden* in London.

Chapter 1

FIFTY FAVOURITE OPERAS

FAVOURITE OPERAS

What makes an opera popular? Obviously, there is the music – but those operas that are clearly favourites and always in the repertoire are extremely musically diverse. There is the question of accessibility, which may explain Puccini, but Wagner and Handel aren't either musically or dramatically necessarily easy to comprehend for the opera beginner. There is the question of staging and performance – though this is highly variable. I have, for instance, seen versions of *Tosca* in which one performer holds the stage and the balance of the drama, simply because they are so breathtaking, you can't take your eyes off them. Callas's *Tosca* (still to be seen on film) set the bar for all later *Tosca*s to follow. But Domingo's Cavaradossi dominated the later Zeffirelli film version. And I have seen one Scarpia so mesmerizing, you began to question Tosca's choice …

So to some extent favourite operas are inevitably a matter of personal preference. There are, though, some that turn up in the repertoire more frequently than others. Here is a round-up of fifty of the most popular that you are likely to find in opera houses and at festivals today.*

---

* (NB Dates refer to the date of the first complete performance.)

L'Incoronazione di Poppea (1642)

(The Coronation of Poppea)
Claudio Monteverdi

First performed in Venice in 1642, *Poppea* was reinstated into the operatic repertoire throughout Europe and the USA during the twentieth century. It was the composer's last opera, written when he was seventy-five, with the help of his gifted librettist, the poet Francesco Busenello. Like all the operas of the time, the subject was classical, but instead of the principals being gods and goddesses, the protagonists – the Emperor Nero and his mistress Poppea – and their emotions were drawn in a newly realistic way. Gods and goddesses do, though, appear in order to comment and advise as the ambitious Poppea persuades Nero to put aside the Empress Octavia and marry her instead. Octavia, though, persuades Poppea's former lover, Ottone, to murder her usurper and it is only the intervention of Venus, Goddess of Love, that prevents him and the opera ends with the lovers triumphant and Poppea crowned. While sometimes transposed to a tenor role, Nero would originally have been sung by a male soprano, usually a *castrato* in Monteverdi's time. Nowadays, the role is generally sung either by a woman or by a countertenor. The music itself is based on what appears to be a rehearsal copy and orchestration now generally reflects the components of the orchestra that prevailed in Monteverdi's day – mostly strings and continuo – with a few more modern elements added in.

Dido and Aeneas (1689)

Henry Purcell

While Purcell wrote plenty of court music, *Dido* is his only true opera, written, oddly enough, for Mr Josias Priest's school for young ladies in Chelsea. It tells the story of Dido, the Queen of Carthage, and her love affair with Aeneas, doomed by the machinations of a wicked Sorceress who tells Aeneas that the gods have decreed he must found the new Troy. As Aeneas sails away to do their bidding, Dido dies of a broken heart. The opera is filled with stately, tragic music but also a surprising number of dances and lively scenes for sailors and witches!

> **DID YOU KNOW?**
> Dido's Lament ('When I am laid in earth') is always played by a
> military band at the Cenotaph on Remembrance Day in Whitehall, in
> London.

The Beggar's Opera (1728)
John Gay

While John Gay is generally credited with *The Beggar's Opera*, he was
mostly responsible for writing the words. The music came from a variety of
sources – folk songs, popular ballads and other operas, including bits of
Handel – and its subject matter was so controversial it was thought it might
be banned (the sequel was). A political satire peopled by highwaymen,
jailers and prostitutes, it could not have strayed further from the operas of
the day, all still mostly interested in classical deities. The Peachum family
receive stolen goods and have a hand in crimes that are far worse. The
daughter Polly secretly marries Captain Macheath, a highwayman. Her
parents had hoped for better things and tell Polly that they will deliver him
up to the law – and he'll be hanged! Macheath is taken off to Newgate Gaol
where he is confronted by Lucy Lockit, the jailer's daughter, and
Macheath's former and now pregnant lover. He insists he is not really
married to Polly and promises to marry her instead. Lucy intercedes with
her father on his behalf. 'How happy could I be with either, Were t'other
dear charmer away!' he sings. Lucy helps Macheath escape and he is next
seen in a gambling den and Lockit and Peachum, tipped off, ensure he's
soon back in chains. Languishing in prison, he's visited not only by Polly
and Lucy but another four wives – at which he calls for the executioner to
be hanged. The story and some of the music has been revived in later
versions by Brecht and Weill and by Benjamin Britten. Brecht's *The
Threepenny Opera* opened almost exactly 200 years after its predecessor and
was equally popular.

Semele (1743)

George Frideric Handel

Many of Handel's operas can now be found in the repertoires of the major opera companies and they are far more widely appreciated than previously, particularly since his tricentenary in 1985. *Semele* is one of Handel's loveliest and musically most inventive operas but *Serse* (*Xerxes*), *Alcina* and *Ariodante* are all wonderful introductions to his work. The libretto was written by the great dramatist William Congreve and the story tells of Semele, the daughter of King Cadmus of Thebes, and her love for the god Jupiter, though she is betrothed to Prince Athamas. On the brink of the wedding, Semele is snatched up by an eagle and sings a lovely aria from a cloud: 'Endless pleasure, endless love Semele enjoys above.' Juno, Jupiter's wife, is not so happy with the arrangement and vows revenge but Jupiter takes Semele to an Arcadian spot and brings her sister Ino to join her. Juno, disguised as Ino, persuades Semele to ask Jupiter not only for immortality for herself but to see him as a god, not in his human disguise. Having promised to grant any request, she tells Jupiter her wish and the blaze of his divine form destroys her. *Semele* is one of the few Handel operas to have had a tenor for the male lead, Jupiter, as the hero in most of his operas was sung by a *castrato*, *castrati* still being very much the stars of the opera in the first half of the eighteenth century.

> **DID YOU KNOW?**
> When Haydn heard *The Messiah*'s Hallelujah Chorus for the first time in Westminster Abbey, he rose to his feet with the crowd, wept, and said, 'He is the master of us all.'

Orfeo ed Euridice (1762)

(Orpheus and Eurydice)
Christoph Gluck

Gluck's masterpiece *Orfeo* was remarkable for its time in its dramatic veracity and characterization. Written originally as a contralto part, the hero *Orfeo*'s part was changed to a tenor for its Parisian debut, Gluck effectively composing it all over again. The story is, of course, that of the bereaved husband Orfeo mourning the loss of his young wife. The gods take pity on him and say he can bring her back from Hades providing he does not turn to look at her until they have crossed the River Styx and returned to the land of the living. He agrees but Eurydice does not know about his promise and so cannot understand why her husband refuses to look at her. Bereft, she declares if he does not look at her she would rather die. Orfeo turns and Eurydice dies. Orfeo sings a beautiful lament that touches the god of love who revives Eurydice yet again.

DID YOU KNOW?
Gluck claimed to be the inventor of musical glasses, giving a concert on them in London in 1746 – though a century earlier there had been an advertisement for 'a concerto upon twenty-six Drinking-Glasses tuned with Spring-Water'.

Le Nozze di Figaro (1786)

(The Marriage of Figaro)
Wolfgang Amadeus Mozart

In a list of this kind, it is impossible to include all of Mozart's operas – which would be the ideal – but *Figaro* is a must, being both a glorious work and one of the most popular and frequently performed in the repertoire. For its time *Figaro* was not only groundbreaking musically, it was also politically shockingly subversive with servants outwitting their masters in a libretto by Lorenzo da Ponte from an original play by Beaumarchais. Above all, though, it is a brilliant comedy of social observation and mistaken identity with a musical complexity never seen before. It starts on Figaro's wedding day. His bride, Susannah, believes the Count, Figaro's master, has his own designs on her. This proves to be correct. Figaro determines to deal with the problem in a plot that sees dastardly intentions confounded, lost parents and children re-united, sopranos playing boys dressed up as girls and a happy ending. Musically, it combines brilliant and memorable arias, one of opera's most famous overtures and complex ensembles for up to nine singers – something never before attempted by any composer.

DID YOU KNOW?

On hearing the opera, the Emperor Joseph II remarked to its composer, 'Too many notes, Mozart.'

Don Giovanni (1787)

Wolfgang Amadeus Mozart

If *Figaro* is a comedy with dramatic undertones, *Don Giovanni* is a drama with plenty of comic moments. Don Giovanni, serial seducer, blasphemer and generally dissolute character, was already well known from various plays famous all over Europe. Da Ponte again wrote the libretto and Mozart created music that ranged from solemn and profoundly moving to comic *opera buffo* songs for the Don's servant, Leporello. The plot turns on the murder by Don Giovanni of the Commendatore, the father of the wronged Donna Anna, in a duel. The Don goes on to seduce other women, including the peasant girl Zerlina on the day of her wedding, and is pursued by others demanding retribution for his seductions. It is the Commendatore – whose statue visits the Don – who brings the final retribution. The Don had mocked the Commendatore and his statue and facetiously invited him to dinner. When the statue arrives, Don Giovanni continues to mock until a fiery pit opens up and demons drag him down to hell.

DID YOU KNOW?
Beethoven, Danzi and Chopin each wrote a series of variations on the duet between the Don and Zerlina, *Là ci darem la mano*.

Die Zauberflöte (1791)

(The Magic Flute)
Wolfgang Amadeus Mozart

Mozart's final opera, written just months before his death, had a libretto in German and pulled together such diverse strings as freemasonry and oriental fairy tales. Tamino falls in love with the portrait of Pamina, daughter of the Queen of the Night, who promises him she will be his bride if he rescues her from the wicked sorcerer, Sarastro. He is given a magic flute to help him on his quest and the comic figure of Papageno, the bird catcher, as his companion. However, when Tamino reaches Sarastro's palace, he discovers he is not a wicked sorcerer at all but a man of wisdom who will guide Tamino on his own spiritual initiation. Sarastro has taken Pamina under his protection away from her evil mother and the two lovers have to prove themselves by going through a series of ordeals. The lovelorn Papageno doesn't manage the ordeals but does find his mate, Papagena.

Fidelio (1805)

Ludwig van Beethoven

Beethoven was the fourth composer to use Jean-Nicolas Bouilly's *Leonore* story as the basis of an opera and his first attempt, called *Leonore*, was a dismal failure. It was not until a reduced and much revised version appeared in 1814 that it became a runaway success. It is the story of Florestan, a Spanish nobleman, who has been unjustly imprisoned by Pizarro, and his rescue by his wife, Leonore, disguised as a boy so she can work for his gaoler. The gaoler's daughter, Marzelline, falls in love with her in her masculine incarnation, inflaming the jealousy of Marzelline's previous lover, Jaquino. When Florestan is about to be murdered, Leonore rescues him, holding Pizarro at gunpoint and the two are re-united.

> **DID YOU KNOW?**
> Beethoven's deafness was due to a severe form of tinnitus and the cause remains unknown. However, it has been the subject of many hypotheses, including typhus, lead poisoning and syphilis.

Il Barbiere di Siviglia (1816)

(The Barber of Seville)
Gioacchino Rossini

Il barbiere is the prequel to Mozart's *Marriage of Figaro* and is the first of Beaumarchais' trio of plays. Again, Figaro is the main protagonist and, again, the overture is instantly recognizable, but all the characters are younger and more innocent – there is none of the poignancy of Mozart's grieving countess. At this stage she is Rosina, ward of Doctor Bartolo, who is planning to marry her. The Count Almaviva, however, has other ideas and with the help of Figaro who is at this point *inter alia* a barber in the city of Seville he plans to abduct her and marry her himself. Figaro comes up with a series of plots for the abduction, which include the Count masquerading as a drunken soldier in search of a billet and an adenoidal singing teacher. There are numerous reversals but the Count eventually snatches Rosina from Bartolo, marrying her moments before he plans to himself. *Il barbiere* is probably one of the most popular operas in the repertoire and it sparkles musically and comically from start to finish.

DID YOU KNOW?
Rossini claimed to have written the opera in just twelve days – and he was not pleased with its first night. It premiered under the title *Almaviva* and was a complete failure, the production sabotaged by whistling and booing by the supporters of Paisiello, who had written the earlier version.

Norma (1831)

Vincenzo Bellini

Norma is a favourite for several reasons – it has expressive, lyrical music of considerable beauty and it is also a tense tragic drama with real insight into the characters. It is set during the Roman occupation of ancient Gaul and Norma is high priestess of the druids. She has broken her vow of chastity for love of Pollione, the Roman pro-consul, but at the outset he confesses to his Centurion Flavio that he no longer loves her, in spite of the two children she has borne him. He has fallen in love with Adalgisa, a virgin of the druid temple. She agrees to leave with Pollone for Rome but goes to confess her sin first to Norma, who is aware she has a rival but does not know her identity. Adalgisa does not name her lover but, when Pollione arrives, it is clear he loves Adalgisa. Norma is prepared to renounce her lover so Adalgisa can marry him, but Adalgisa promises instead to remind Pollione of his duty to Norma. But Adalgisa's plea fails, Norma is furious and she calls the warriors of Gaul to fight the Romans. Pollione is captured breaking into the temple to carry off Adalgisa – the penalty for which is death. Norma substitutes herself as the victim, telling the Gauls she is a perjured virgin of the priesthood. She enters the pyre on which she is to burn to death – and Pollione joins her, overwhelmed by her sacrifice.

L'Elisir d'Amore (1832)

(The Elixir of Love)
Gaetano Donizetti

Many of Donizetti's operas were historical and tragic (*Anna Bolena*, *Lucrezia Borgia*, *Maria Stuarda* and what many consider his masterpiece, *Lucia di Lammermoor*) but he wrote two that can both reduce an audience to tears of laughter and touch them, too, with their utterly beautiful melodies. *L'Elisir d'Amore* is the comic tale of a besotted young peasant, Nemorino, who has fallen for Adina, a wealthy and beautiful farmer. His rival is Sergeant Belcore and Nemorino feels he has no chance with Adina until the quack Doctor Dulcamara arrives in the village, selling his elixir of love, which, he promises the lovelorn youth, will make Adina his. The elixir is, in fact, a bottle of cheap Bordeaux and Nemorino becomes a party animal under its influence. Adina, piqued by his apparent lack of interest, engages herself immediately to Belcore. Nemorino buys a second bottle of the elixir but to pay for it has to enlist in Belcore's troop. Adina realizes she has preferred Nemorino all along and buys him out of the army. Nemorino turns out to be the heir to his rich uncle and Dulcamara's elixir becomes so highly sought after that he sells the lot at a tremendous profit. The plot and music gallop along and are utterly charming, the high point being Nemorino's hauntingly beautiful 'Una furtive lagrima'.

DID YOU KNOW?

Donizetti was overcome with the rapturous reception of *L'Elisir d'Amore*. He wrote to his mother of the review in the Milan newspapers: 'The *Gazzetta* says too many good things; too many, believe me, too many!'

Lucia di Lammermoor (1835)

Gaetano Donizetti

Some of Donizetti's most memorable music – from tragic to scintillating – appears in *Lucia* and it is often cited as his finest opera. There are numerous high points, including the sextet at the end of the second act when Lucia has signed the marriage contract, and, of course, Lucia's famous mad scene. The plot tells the story of a doomed love between Lucia and Edgar of Ravenswood. Lucia's brother Henry, knowing nothing of this, arranges to marry her to Lord Arthur Bucklaw in order to shore up his fortune and disentangle himself from a political mistake. Henry forges a letter from Edgar to show Lucy he is unfaithful and persuades her to marry Lord Arthur. Edgar returns, believes her to have betrayed him and curses the house of Lammermoor. Henry challenges him to a duel but Lucy, driven to madness by her sorrow, murders her husband and dies of a broken heart. The next morning, Edgar awaits Henry for the duel, but sees instead Lucy's mourners coming from the Castle of Lammermoor. He dies, the last of his race, by his own hand in the churchyard where his ancestors are buried.

Don Pasquale (1843)

Gaetano Donizetti

Don Pasquale is Donizetti's other great comic opera. The story begins with the wealthy Don Pasquale's plans to marry – the question is who. His friend Malatesta offers his 'sister', a quiet, innocent girl brought up in a convent. This is really Norina, a young widow, no relation to Malatesta, who is actually planning to marry Ernesto, Don Pasquale's nephew. Though he doesn't know Ernesto's beloved, he disapproves on principle of his nephew marrying and threatens to disinherit him if he does. When Ernesto discovers it is Norina his uncle plans to marry, he is distraught – not realizing that it is a plot devised by Norina and Malatesta to secure her marriage with Ernesto. Don Pasquale and Norina meet and he is enraptured by her docility until the marriage contract is signed and she suddenly turns into a spitfire, demanding more servants, insulting Don Pasquale's age and girth and going out to the theatre – with Ernesto. In despair at the prospect of marrying this harridan, Don Pasquale asks for Malatesta's advice in a hilarious comic duet. The lovers meet in the garden where Ernesto sings a beautiful serenade to Norina. They are discovered by Don Pasquale and Malatesta and the latter manages to calm the ruffled feathers in a finale which promises the marriage of Norina and Ernesto – to the relief of Don Pasquale.

Rigoletto (1851)

Giuseppe Verdi

One of Verdi's indisputable masterpieces, *Rigoletto* was written in just forty days and became an immediate favourite. It has three great roles – Caruso made his extraordinary debut at the Metropolitan Opera in New York playing the Duke – and some truly soaring music. It also has an intense and tragic plot that centres on Rigoletto, the court jester of the Duke of Mantua, who has helped his libidinous master in his many seductions. Away from the court, though, Rigoletto keeps his daughter Gilda – of whom his many enemies at court know nothing – in the strictest seclusion. One of them does discover her existence and abducts her (with Rigoletto's unwitting help) for the Duke. Realizing what has happened, he decides his only course is to murder the Duke and engages a thug, Sparafucile, to do the deed. Sparafucile's sister Maddalena persuades the Duke to meet her at a lonely inn but falls in love with him herself and persuades her brother to let him live – providing another body can be found to give to Rigoletto. The jester has rescued his daughter and takes her to the inn so she can see for herself (as she is in fact also in love with the Duke) how faithless he is.

DID YOU KNOW?

At the first night of *Rigoletto*, the hump-backed jester was played by Felice Varesi, who was having trouble with his hump and suffered a panic attack. Verdi gave him a shove from the wings and he tumbled on to the stage – much to the amusement of the audience.

When she hears the plot, she decides to save the Duke by sacrificing her own life and is stabbed on entering the inn. When Rigoletto comes to collect the Duke's body it is actually Gilda who is in the sack and her father opens it to find her on the verge of death.

La Traviata (1853)

Giuseppe Verdi

Based on Alexandre Dumas' play *La Dame aux Camelias*, *La Traviata* is the story of a courtesan, Violetta, whose extravagant lifestyle is funded by her lover, the Baron Douphol. The opera opens in the middle of her party and amid the many guests is Alfredo Germont, who declares himself in love with Violetta – an announcement she does not take too seriously. However, when she is overcome with the signs of the consumption that will later take hold, Alfredo remains with her and declares his love again and this time she listens and seems to be touched by it until she remembers who she is and declares herself incapable of true love. But as the curtain opens for the second act she has clearly changed her mind and the two are living together in the country, deeply happy but with ever-increasing money problems. Violetta has been selling her jewels and when Alfredo finds out he goes to Paris to buy them back. While he is away, Alfredo's father comes to plead with her to leave Alfredo so his daughter can marry without scandal. In a moving duet Violetta agrees, but making him promise he will tell Alfredo the truth of her love for him on her death, which she fears will come soon. Knowing it will be hard to convince him she does not love him, she goes back to Baron Douphol and her old life. Alfredo turns up at the party where Violetta is a guest with the Baron and gambles heavily. Violetta begs Alfredo to leave, fearing the Baron will demand a duel, but Alfredo calls the other guests into the room, insults Violetta and throws his winnings at her in payment for their time in the country. The final act takes place in Violetta's bedroom, where she is close to death. Alfredo, informed by his father of the true story of Violetta's sacrifice, rushes in and believes she can recover. For a moment it seems she rallies, then it is all over and she dies in Alfredo's arms.

DID YOU KNOW?
When *La Traviata* was premiered, it was a total flop. Verdi wrote to a friend, '*La Traviata* last night was a failure. My fault or the singers'? Time will tell.' This was somewhat disingenuous on Verdi's part as he felt the singers were cast badly – in particular the overweight soprano singing the consumptive Violetta.

Faust (1859)

Charles Francois Gounod

Gounod's opera uses only a part of Goethe's masterpiece for its plot, the selling of Faust's soul to Mephistopheles in return for eternal youth and Faust's doomed love affair with Marguerite – it is known in Germany, in fact, as *Margarethe*. At the start of the opera Marguerite already has an admirer, Siebel, a friend of her brother, Valentine, but Mephistopheles finds ways to part them to leave the way clear to Faust. Beguiled by Faust's gift of pearls, Marguerite pledges her love to him – watched over by Mephistopheles. Faust deserts Marguerite, leaving her pregnant, and goaded by Mephistopheles, Faust kills her brother Valentine in a street sword fight. Marguerite is sent to prison, condemned for the murder of their child, and Faust visits her along with Mephistopheles. In a magnificent trio, Marguerite calls upon the angels to save her, and they bear her away as she dies. Faust is left to await his own infernal destiny.

DID YOU KNOW?
Faust was almost the cause of a duel. A critic announced Gounod could not have been the composer, Gounod challenged him, and he was forced to withdraw his allegation. Many years later the story was revived by acquaintances of Gounod's saying he had stolen the score from a young genius who had died in a lunatic asylum.

Les Troyens (1863)

(The Trojans)
Hector Berlioz

Berlioz is, depending on your point of view, the greatest French composer of operas or a deeply flawed genius. The most often performed of his works, *Les Troyens* is a gigantic work in length and spectacle when staged in full – but Berlioz himself never saw the complete opera performed. Donald Gould in *A Short History of Opera* (OUP) described it as 'the Latin counterpart of Wagner's Teutonic Ring' and there are many difficulties in staging it – a massive chorus, several ballets, many scene changes. The subject itself, the Trojan War, is of course of mythic proportions. Berlioz takes up the story at the point that the wooden horse is left behind by the apparently defeated Greeks, continues with the story of Aeneas and his escape to Carthage and his love for Queen Dido, whom he deserts for duty and destiny.

Les Pêcheurs de Perles (1863)

(The Pearl Fishers)
Georges Bizet

Bizet's second most famous opera is set in ancient Ceylon and revolves around a love triangle: two pearl fishermen, Zurga and Nadir, have both in the past fallen in love with Leila, a Brahmin priestess, whom they had seen in the temple. They fought over her but she left and they once again became friends. Now she has returned as the inviolate virgin priestess for the pearl fishermen. All of the old passions are once more inflamed. Nadir and Leila reaffirm their love but, overheard by the high priest Nourabad, they face death for this sacrilege. Zurga is jealous but discovers that long ago Leila had saved his life and in gratitude he helps them escape. The opera is filled with the superb melodies that Bizet is renowned for, the most famous being the duet for Zurga and Nadir, among many other seductively beautiful moments.

Tristan und Isolde (1865)

Richard Wagner

Wagner changed opera forever and *Tristan und Isolde* is widely regarded as the greatest setting of a love story in the history of opera – passion, death and surging, extraordinary music. The plot is based on medieval legend and was adapted by Wagner. It begins on board a ship: Tristan is taking Isolde to marry his uncle, Mark, King of Cornwall. Tristan and Isolde are, though, in love with each other, Isolde having nursed Tristan back to health after he was wounded in combat. Both, however, believe their love to be unrequited. Isolde resolves to both kill Tristan and die herself and they share a death potion. However, Isolde's attendant Brangäne has switched bottles and it is a love potion that they share. The music soars and they know their love cannot be denied. In Cornwall they meet secretly but are surprised by the King and his retinue and, in a fight, Tristan is dangerously wounded by one of the King's knights. Tristan leaves the court and returns to his home. Isolde arrives only in time for Tristan to die in her arms and, gazing at him with the remembered ecstasy of their love, she follows him into death.

A LOVELORN COMPOSER

In a letter to Franz Liszt in December 1854 when he was first thinking about the opera, Wagner wrote:

Never in my life having enjoyed the true happiness of love I shall erect a memorial to this loveliest of all dreams in which, from the first to the last, love shall, for once, find utter repletion. I have devised in my mind a *Tristan und Isolde*, the simplest, yet most full-blooded musical conception imaginable, and with the 'black flag' that waves at the end I shall cover myself over – to die.

Aida (1871)

Giuseppe Verdi

Aida was commissioned for the Italian Theatre in Cairo by Ismail Pasha, Khedive (Viceroy) of Egypt and it was an immediate success there and indeed everywhere it was staged in Europe and America, where its dramatic setting of ancient Egypt captivated audiences. So, too, did the music, which ranged from romantic arias to Egyptian temple chants and sweeping choral music. The plot concerns the love of Aida, an Ethiopian princess but now a slave to Amneris, the daughter of Egypt's king, and Radames, a soldier in the Egyptian army. Radames is entirely unaware that Amneris herself is in love with him, too. The goddess Isis chooses Radames to lead the Egyptian army in battle against the Ethiopians – led by Aida's father. Aida is cruelly torn, but Amneris, seeing how Radames looks at Aida, is consumed by jealousy. Radames is blessed by the gods to the accompaniment of harps and chanting priestesses and goes off to war. News soon comes that Radames is victorious and Aida fears both for her father's and her lover's safety. Amneris tricks Aida into confessing her love and the two watch the triumphal march of the army and its booty. Radames is given his victor's crown and the king's promise to grant his dearest wish. First Radames asks for the prisoners to be brought in and Aida cries out when she sees her father, Amonasro, the Ethiopian king. However, the Egyptian army believe the Ethiopian king to be dead and Amonasro pleads for the lives of the prisoners. Radames seconds the plea and the king grants it, also giving him the hand of his daughter Amneris in marriage. Radames cannot refuse. The third act begins with Aida waiting for a secret meeting with Radames but surprised first by her father who persuades her to find out his campaign plans against the Ethiopians so her country can be saved. Reluctantly, she finally agrees. Radames meets her and has a plan of his own – he will win the next campaign against the Ethiopians and beg the king in return for Aida as his bride. She implores him instead to run away with her but also draws out of him the planned route of the army. Amonasro hears it all but so does Amneris and with Radames' help Amonasro and Aida flee. The final act sees Amneris try to persuade Radames to plead his innocence but he refuses as, without Aida, he would rather die. His sentence is to be buried alive – but Aida, knowing this would be his fate, hides in the dungeon before him and, reunited in love, they die together. For magnificence, spectacle and a three-hanky ending, there is nothing to beat *Aida*.

> **DID YOU KNOW?**
> A popular musical version of *Aida* was written by Elton John and Tim Rice in 1988 using the story but not the music. It was not a success.

Boris Godunov (1874)

Modest Petrovich Mussorgsky

For many, *Boris* is the best of all Russian operas. Its deft characterization, splendid bass role, the magnificent chorus and the fascinating – if confusing – period of Russian history it portrays all make it deservedly

> **DID YOU KNOW?**
> *Boris* was re-written by Rimsky-Korsakov after the composer's death and it did make it more appealing to the public taste, though now it is the original that is more often used. At the time he explained his re-writing of the scores thus:
>
> They were very defective, teeming with clumsy, disconnected harmonies, shocking part-writing, amazingly illogical modulations or intolerably long stretches without ever a modulation, and bad scoring ... what is needed is an edition for practical and artistic purposes, suitable for performances and for those who wish to admire Mussorgsky's genius, not to study his idiosyncrasies and sins against art.

popular. The plot begins in 1598 when Boris Godunov murders Dimitri, the heir to the Russian throne, and is himself crowned as Tsar. However, a young monk, Grigory, goes to Poland and claims to be the Tsarevich Dimitri. He is accepted, marries the Princess Marina and marches on Moscow at the head of the Polish army. Boris is meanwhile racked with guilt and suffering from hallucinations and dies telling his son he is the lawful heir. Dimitri, though, usurps power as Boris did before him and a poor simpleton is left to mourn the plight of the Russian people.

Die Fledermaus (1874)

(The Bat)
Johann Strauss

Die Fledermaus is undoubtedly the most delightful of all the Viennese operettas. It has wonderful melodies (lots of waltzes, naturally) and a fizzing comic plot. This centres on Gabriel von Eisenstein and his wife Rosalinda. The husband has to serve a short prison sentence – but first, unbeknown to his wife, he is going with his friend Dr Falke to the party given by Prince Orlofsky. Falke is, though, plotting revenge on his friend who played a trick on him, leaving him after a previous party dressed as a bat (hence the title) asleep in the street. However, Rosalinda is also going to the party, wearing a mask. Finally, so is Adele, the family's maid. Von Eisenstein sets off for prison – rather oddly in evening dress – and Alfred, an old admirer of Rosalinda, arrives moments later. He is enjoying Alfred's dinner when Frank the prison governor arrives to escort Von Eisenstein to jail. To safeguard her reputation, Rosalinda identifies Alfred as her husband and he goes to prison in Von Eisenstein's stead. At the party, Von Eisenstein recognizes his maid but not his wife, who is masquerading as a Hungarian countess. He attempts to seduce her but the seduction goes wrong and the countess ends up with his watch before introducing a Czardas (a plaintive traditional Hungarian song). After a ballet, the famous *Die Fledermaus* waltz plays the party to its close – with Von Eisenstein's departure for prison. The final act is set in the prison and is a mêlée of mistaken identities and two Von Eisensteins. Gradually all are unmasked and accept their roles as the butts of many jokes but are reconciled in blaming all their misdemeanours on champagne.

Carmen (1875)

Georges Bizet

One of the most popular operas of all time, *Carmen* combines a plot of doomed love with an electric score, brilliantly inventive and exhilarating throughout. The story is, of course, that of Carmen, the irresistible but fickle gypsy. She seduces Don Jose not only away from his fiancée, the pure Micaela, but his career as a soldier – he is completely undone by the end of her seductive Habanera 'L'amour est un oiseau rebelle'. But Don Jose has a rival – Escamillo the bullfighter. However, Carmen is still enamoured of Don Jose and he is just as besotted with her so he leaves Seville to join her band of gypsies in the mountains. The second act takes place in the mountains where Carmen reads her fortune in the cards – death. In the meantime, Micaela has made her way in spite of her terror to the gypsy encampment to try to persuade Don Jose to come back, but before she finds him, Escamillo does. The two men fight but the other gypsies return and Escamillo invites them all to the bullfight – though it is clear it is Carmen he wants there. Micaela reappears and begs Don Jose to at least return to see his mother, who is dying of a broken heart. The final act opens with Carmen and Escamillo acclaimed by the crowds on their way to the bullfight. The toreador prepares to enter the arena but Carmen, still in the street outside, finds herself face to face with Don Jose. He pleads with her to leave with him but she refuses and says she can no longer love him. They quarrel against the noise of the bullfight and when Carmen finally admits she loves Escamillo, Don Jose plunges his knife into her just as the crowd acclaims Escamillo's triumph in the bullring. Although recognized as a masterpiece today, when it was premiered at the Opéra-Comique in Paris it flopped, and this wound to Bizet's pride was thought to be a contributing factor to his death just three months later.

Der Ring des Nibelungen (1876)

(The Ring of the Nibelung)
Richard Wagner

Although parts of the Ring Cycle had appeared earlier, it was only in 1876 that the complete work was performed in Bayreuth. It consists of four separate parts – Das Rheingold (*The Rhine Gold*), *Die Walküre* (*The Valkyrie*), *Siegfried* and *Gotterdammerung* (*Twilight of the Gods*). Wagner had actually started working on the idea for the Ring Cycle in 1848 but it was only after he obtained the patronage of King Ludwig II of Bavaria that he was able to produce this and other works on the scale he desired. And the scale was epic – musically, scenically, emotionally and in terms of sheer time. *The Rhine Gold* tells how Alberich, the Nibelung dwarf, steals the gold of the Rhinemaidens and makes it into a magic ring, with which he intends to make himself the master of the world. Meanwhile, Wotan, chief among the gods and, like Alberich, a symbol of greed for wealth and power, steals the ring and the rest of the gold to give in payment to the giants Fasolt and Fafner, who have built the gods' new home, Valhalla. They give Freia, goddess of eternal youth, in return but immediately quarrel about who will keep the ring – fulfilling the curse Alberich has put upon it. Fafner kills Fasolt, the gods enter Valhalla and the Rhinemaidens lament the loss of their treasure. *The Valkyrie* opens with Siegmund hiding from his enemies in Hunding's hut, where he is found by Sieglinde, Hunding's wife. Immediately drawn to each other – they are, in fact, brother and sister – Sieglinde shows Siegmund the sword left in a tree trunk by Wotan that can only be drawn out by a hero. Siegmund frees the sword, the two embrace and run away together. Siegmund and Hunding fight, watched over by the gods. Fricka tells Wotan he must side with Hunding, the wronged husband. Brünnhilde, Wotan's favourite daughter and Valkyrie warrior, supports Siegmund. Both warriors die and Brünnhilde takes the pregnant Sieglinde and the remains of Siegmund's broken sword to safety but is punished by her father, who sends her to sleep on a rock surrounded by fire, only to be awoken by a true hero. Siegfried – the son of Siegmund and Sieglinde – learns the story of his birth from Mime, who has brought him up in a cave in the forest. Wotan in disguise quizzes Mime about Siegfried and prophesies the sword will only be forged again by a true hero. Siegfried, in spite of Mime's attempts on his life, forges the sword and kills Fafner – now in the form of a dragon guarding the Rhinegold. He goes in search of Brünnhilde and walks through the magic fire to claim her as his wife. In *Gotterdammerung*, the final part of the cycle, Siegfried has given the ring to Brünnhilde and goes to find Hagen, Alberich's son, who lives with his half-brother Gunther and half-sister Gutrune. Hagen drugs Siegfried who, as a result, forgets Brünnhilde and resolves to marry Gutrune. Hagen then sends him to fetch Brünnhilde so he can marry her himself. Brought to the brink of the horrific double wedding and filled with hate for Siegfried at his seeming treachery, Brünnhilde plots his death. Hagen kills Siegfried and then Gunther in yet another quarrel over the ring. Brünnhilde, discovering she and Siegfried have been victims of a plot, has a funeral pyre built for Siegfried and when it is lit rides her horse into the flames. Hagen tries to snatch the ring from her but the Rhine overflows its banks and he is dragged into its depths by the Rhinemaidens, one of whom has also seized the ring. In the background, Valhalla is consumed by fire. The old order passes away and the human era dawns.

A RING PASSED ON?

When Tolkein's *Lord of the Rings* was published, some critics thought there was a strong link to Wagner's work. Others argued that they had simply referred to some of the same sources. Tolkein said, 'Both rings were round and there the resemblance ceases.'

Samson et Dalila (1877)

(Samson and Delilha)

Camille Saint-Saëns

First conceived of as an oratorio, *Samson et Dalila* became Saint-Saëns' most popular opera. It is based on the biblical story in which the Hebrew warrior Samson leads a successful revolt against his people's Philistine masters. The Philistine Dalila, with a group of other maidens, goes to pay homage to Samson, and Dalila, his erstwhile lover, bewitches him all over again. She sings languorously beautiful arias but admits to herself that, since he left her, she hates him and she determines, encouraged by the High Priest, to discover the secret of his strength. Samson resists all he can – but in the end he reveals his power and Dalila cuts off his hair. Blinded, Samson is left in a dungeon to torment himself with his folly and despair. Philistine soldiers drag him out to be displayed at the temple where the Philistines are celebrating. Dalila mocks him again and the seductive Bacchanale follows. Samson prays for strength and he pulls down the pillars of the temple, which crashes down on to the Philistines.

Eugene Onegin (1879)

Peter Ilitsch Tchaikovsky

Onegin is based on Pushkin's classic poem and has music that soars to poetic heights – including, of course, Tatiana's letter scene, a tour de force for sopranos. Sisters Olga and Tatiana are at home at their mother's house when Olga's fiancé Lensky arrives with his friend, Onegin. Tatiana falls violently in love with him and writes a letter declaring her feelings. Onegin, however, rejects her, declaring love and marriage are not for him. Later, at a ball, Onegin flirts with Olga out of boredom and Lensky challenges him to a duel. Lensky is killed and Onegin flees abroad. Six years later, Onegin has returned to Russia and attends a ball in St Petersburg. Prince Gremin arrives with his beautiful wife – Onegin discovers to his amazement it is Tatiana. He also discovers he is hopelessly in love with her. He sends her a letter and Tatiana admits she does still love him but would never leave her husband and Onegin realizes he has lost her forever.

Les Contes d'Hoffman (1881)

(The Tales of Hoffman)
Jacques Offenbach

Offenbach's masterpiece and only romantic opera opens and closes in a wine cellar where the drunken poet Hoffman is regaling his friends with his three great loves. The next three acts reveal them to be, first, Olympia, who turns out to be an animated doll (the same story is told in the ballet *Coppélia*). The second act features the consumptive singer Antonia, who dies when goaded by Dr Miracle to continue singing against the orders of her doctor. And the third, set in Venice, introduces the courtesan Giulietta, who steals his reflection, and the unforgettable barcarole.

DID YOU KNOW?
Offenbach died three months before the rapturous reception of his most ambitious work.

Lakmé (1883)

Leo Delibes

Delibes' masterpiece features some of the most seductive and sumptuous music in French opera, including the captivating 'Flower Duet'. It is set in nineteenth-century India and is the story of Lakmé, the daughter of Nilakantha, a Brahmin priest, who hates the invading British with a passion having been forbidden to practise his religion. Lakmé has left her jewellery in the temple garden, where it is found by Gerald, a British officer, and his friends. Gerald, left alone, wonders what the owner can be like and hides when he hears Lakmé returning with her slave Mallika. Gerald is infatuated with her on sight but Lakmé tells him he must leave or face death, and her father arrives to confirm he wants vengeance on the infidel who has profaned the temple by his presence. Nilakantha devises a plot to trap Gerald. In the bazaar, he tells Lakmé to sing, but when she sees Gerald (with his fiancée Ellen) she faints. Nilakantha recognizes him as the enemy. Later, Gerald rushes back to Lakmé's side and she declares her love, but they are disturbed by a religious procession during which Gerald is stabbed. He is only slightly injured and Lakmé takes him to a secret hiding place. Although the lovers are happy, Gerald's friend Frederic has followed them and, when Gerald is alone, tells him he must come with his regiment, who are moving that night. When Lakmé returns she realizes that Gerald is distracted, fears his love is fading and takes poison. She dies as they promise they will love each other for all eternity.

Cavalleria Rusticana (1890)

(Rustic Chivalry)
Pietro Mascagni

This one-act opera is based on a short story by Giovanni Verga and tells the tragic story of Santuzza and her betrayal in love by Turiddu with Lola, who is not only a heartless flirt but also married to Alfio. Santuzza in an impassioned duet tells Turiddu she forgives him and still loves him but he spurns her and she tells Alfio of his wife's infidelity. There follows a short but beautiful intermezzo and then the action resumes with Turiddu buying drinks for everyone in his mother's wine shop. Alfio arrives and challenges Turiddu and he kills him with his stiletto. The women – Turiddu's mother and Santuzza – are left to mourn at the end of a typical Sicilian tragedy.

Pagliacci (1892)

(The Strolling Players)
Ruggiero Leoncavallo

Pagliacci is a short opera often teamed with another in performance, usually *Cavalleria Rusticana* (see above), and features a play within a play that reflects the relationships and troubles of the players. The band of strolling players is performing in the Italian village of Montalto, much to the excitement of the locals. Canio and Nedda are married but in the play Nedda plays Columbine to Beppe's Harlequin. It is Tonio, the clown, however, who is desperately in love with Nedda but she spurns him and he promises revenge. It is, though, yet another man, Silvio, a local villager, who persuades Nedda to run away with him. Tonio overhears their plans and tells Canio. Nedda refuses to reveal the name of her lover but the other players believe he will reveal himself during their performance and go to prepare. Canio then sings 'Vesti la giubba' ('On with the motley') – the opera's most famous aria – when he laments his inner grief that he must cover in his comic performance. The show itself is classic *commedia dell'arte* and plays out Nedda's infidelity to Canio, now a buffoon husband and cuckold. Then Canio can bear it no longer and – in character, the audience believes – he demands the name of his wife's lover. Nedda flees into the audience, chased by Canio, who stabs her to death.

La Bohème (1896)

(The Bohemian Girl)
Giacomo Puccini

One of Puccini's most loved operas, *La Bohème* manages to combine high spirits and comedy with soaring melodies of love and death. It is set in the Latin Quarter in Paris and opens in the garret where four friends live – Rodolfo the poet, Marcello the painter, Colline the philosopher and Schaunard the musician. Mimi, a seamstress, lives in the same building and meets Rodolfo. They immediately fall in love but Mimi has a frail beauty that presages consumption. The two go out to join the other friends at the Café Momus, where they are joined by Musetta (Marcello's former love), who is with the old – but wealthy – Alcindoro. Musetta and Marcello make up, leaving Alcindoro to pay everyone's bill. The third act sees a rift between Rodolfo and Mimi – he is jealous, but accuses her of heartlessness. It is Christmas and the four friends are making merry in the garret – despite their poverty – when Musetta tells them Mimi is dying. She brings her in and Mimi and Rodolfo again find they love each other, but it is too late and Mimi dies.

Tosca (1900)

Giacomo Puccini

One of Puccini's most dramatic operas, *Tosca* tells the story of the love of the singer, Tosca, for the painter Cavaradossi, which is thwarted by the desire of the Chief of Police, Scarpia, who wants Tosca for himself. Tosca's fatal flaw is jealousy and it is inflamed when she comes to see Cavaradossi in the church of Sant'Andrea della Valle in Rome, where he is painting Mary Magdalene. She fears he is basing it on another woman, but Cavaradossi is anxious because he is hiding Angelotti, a political prisoner. Scarpia feeds Tosca's jealousy, claiming to have found her feared rival's fan on Cavaradossi's easel. And he soliloquizes in a superb aria, full of increasing and sinister power, his plan to execute Cavaradossi and have Tosca for his own. The second act takes place in Scarpia's apartments in the Farnese Palace where Cavaradossi is being questioned about Angelotti. Tosca is summoned and embraces Cavaradossi who warns her not to tell Scarpia anything of the political prisoner hiding in his villa. Cavaradossi is taken to another room – he can be heard groaning from torture – while Scarpia questions Tosca about Angelotti's whereabouts. Finally, she tells Scarpia what he wants to know to save Cavaradossi from further torture. But Scarpia prepares to sign the painter's death warrant and tells Tosca the only way to save him is to give herself to him. Tosca agrees if Scarpia will give a bill of safe conduct for her and for Cavaradossi so they can escape Rome the next day. Scarpia agrees and Tosca stabs him. At dawn on the Castle Sant'Angelo, Cavaradossi is preparing for his execution when Tosca comes to tell him it will be merely a mock execution and they can then escape together. The firing squad arrives – but it was not a mock execution after all. Scarpia has tricked Tosca at the last and she throws herself from the roof to her death.

DID YOU KNOW?
Tosca was not an immediate hit and one musicologist, Joseph Kerman, dismissed it as a 'shabby little shocker'.

Rusalka (1901)

(The Water Nymph)
Antonín Dvořák

Dvořák set the folk tale *Rusalka* to lyrically beautiful music that ensured the opera a place in the repertoire. Rusalka, a water nymph, has fallen in love with a handsome prince and longs to become human. Jezibaba, the witch, agrees to help her, but makes her accept that if the prince turns out to be false to her, they will both be damned forever. The prince discovers her in human form and is enchanted by her, taking her back to his palace. But Rusalka cannot speak and the prince's subjects fear her, suspecting witchcraft. A foreign princess comes to the palace and the prince abandons Rusalka. Rusalka is now condemned to wander as a will-o'-the-wisp unless, Jezibaba tells her, she removes the curse by shedding human blood. The Prince makes his way back to the forest where he first saw Rusalka and begs her forgiveness but she tells him, were she to embrace him, he would die. He begs for a kiss and dies in her arms.

Pelléas et Mélisande (1902)

Claude Debussy

Debussy's beautiful and lyrical music is better known in his piano, orchestral and ballet works, but it transfers here to the voice (and the orchestra) to magical effect. The story is taken from Maeterlinck's play of the same name and Debussy's music is true to the play's sometimes obscure symbolism. Golaud, the grandson of King Arkel of Allemonde, finds Mélisande sitting by a spring, a strange, almost unearthly girl. He takes her out of the dark forest and marries her, though he still knows little about her. The couple go to King Arkel's castle but Mélisande finds it gloomy and frightening. Later Mélisande is walking in the park with Pelléas, Golaud's brother, when she is drawn towards a fountain and the ring her husband has given her slips into the water. At that moment, Golaud's horse shies and throws him. Mélisande is nursing him when he discovers his ring is missing. When Pelléas comes to take leave before a journey, Golaud sees there is something between his brother and his wife, and he warns him to keep away. Yet, in spite of setting his child to spy on them, the husband can find nothing to upbraid his wife for. Nevertheless, Golaud is consumed with jealousy and kills Pelléas. Mélisande delivers a child then she, too, dies.

DID YOU KNOW?
The piano teacher of Debussy – composer of *Clair du lune* – declared 'He doesn't much care for the piano.'

Madama Butterfly (1904)

Giacomo Puccini

Puccini's most famous opera had a rocky start, booed at its premiere and much revised over the next couple of years. The plot was the tragic tale of a marriage between Cio-Cio-San, known as Butterfly, and Lieutenant BF Pinkerton of the US Navy in Nagasaki. But, though Butterfly believes this to be a genuine marriage, Pinkerton tells Sharpless, the American Consul, much to the latter's dismay, that this is a 'Japanese marriage' – a temporary arrangement. Butterfly is, in fact, in love with Pinkerton and has even renounced her religion before entering into her new life with him, though this will mean her relatives will cast her off. There is a long and touching love scene between the newlyweds, but when the curtain rises on the next act, Butterfly is alone but for her servant Suzuki, impoverished, but dreaming for her husband's return. Pinkerton does return but with a 'real' American wife. Sharpless tries to persuade her that she has been abandoned and she should listen to another wealthy suitor who wants to marry her. But Butterfly brings out her little boy – Pinkerton's son – and assures him that he will make her husband hurry back. Pinkerton's ship sails into the harbour and Butterfly prepares to welcome him but she waits for hours and the humming song that accompanies her vigil makes it poignant in the extreme. Morning breaks and Butterfly is still watching. Suzuki persuades her to rest and Pinkerton arrives with Sharpless, finally sees how badly he has treated Butterfly and flees, leaving Sharpless to face Butterfly. When she understands at last what has happened she tells Pinkerton's new wife she can take the boy. Butterfly kills herself with her father's sword, dying as Pinkerton arrives to claim his son.

DID YOU KNOW?
Butterfly is one of the world's most popular operas and ranks as the number one most performed opera in the United States.

Salome (1905)

Richard Strauss

A translation of Oscar Wilde's poem formed the libretto of *Salome*. The step-daughter of Herod is known to be depraved and she is the subject of the soldiers' talk outside the palace. They are silenced by the thundering voice of Jokanaan (John the Baptist) in his dank prison. Salome comes out on to the terrace, curious to see the caged Prophet, and so he is brought out, dressed in rags. Jokanaan curses Herod and his wife Herodias – Salome's mother. Salome, though, is fascinated and she attempts to seduce him. Jokanaan rejects her and the court joins her on the terrace. Herod makes clear his lust for his step-daughter and asks her to dance for the company. She only agrees when he promises to give her whatever she asks. She performs the dance of the seven veils and then demands the head of the Prophet. Herod offers her every substitute he can think of, but in the end, agrees. The Prophet is killed and his head brought to her on a silver charger, prompting her to caress it in a frenzy of lust. Even Herod is disgusted and orders his guards to crush her to death beneath their shields.

Der Rosenkavalier (1911)

(The Knight of the Rose)
Richard Strauss

One of the most popular of twentieth-century operas, *Der Rosenkavalier* is a favourite in most repertoires. It not only has a wealth of memorable waltz tunes for a huge orchestra and charmingly comic moments, it is lifted to quite another level by the character of the Marschallin. It opens in the bedroom of the Marschallin, where she has spent a night of passion with the young Count Octavian, her husband the Field Marshal being away. He is seventeen, she is thirty-two, and she worries that he will look for younger sweethearts when he leaves her room. They are alarmed by the arrival of the boorish Baron Ochs, who is quite smitten by the Marschallin's new chambermaid – actually Octavian in disguise. He asks the Marschallin to arrange to take the traditional silver rose to Sophie, a young woman he has decided to wed. Left alone, she remembers her own youth and considers Sophie's plight. She decides Octavian will take the silver rose. Sophie is an innocent, sweet girl but her father has decided Baron Ochs will be a suitable match, as the marriage will restore his own fortunes. Octavian arrives to deliver the rose and the two are immediately attracted to each other. The Baron himself arrives and Sophie is dismayed to find him such an oaf. Octavian and the Baron quarrel and Octavian determines to reveal the Baron in his true colours. Octavian, dressed again in maid's clothes, arranges an assignation with the Baron. A hilarious scene in which the Baron twists and turns to avoid his fate is brought to an end by the arrival of the Marschallin. She realizes what has happened, unites the young lovers and gracefully gives up her prior claim, and there follows an exquisite trio for the three female voices (Octavian is also sung by a soprano).

Duke Bluebeard's Castle (1918)

(A kékszakállú Herceg Vára)
Béla Bartók

Bartók's opera is unusual on many levels, not least in that it has just two singers, Bluebeard and his wife, Judith, and it lasts under an hour. The music is vivid and dramatic, in spite of the fact that there is little in the way of action. The set is a large round room with seven doors but no windows, so when Bluebeard leads in his new wife, she wants to open the doors to let in the light. In so doing she finds a torture chamber, an armoury, a treasury, a garden and the entrance to Bluebeard's Kingdom. Behind the next door is water, signifying tears. Bluebeard gives her the seventh key reluctantly and she discovers his three former wives. She joins them behind the seventh door, leaving Bluebeard alone once more.

Katya Kabanova (1921)

Leos Janacek

It is widely assumed that *Katya Kabanova* was inspired by Janacek's late love (he was sixty-three, she was twenty-five) for Kamila Stösslová and, in it, he does contrast the older matriarchal generation with the young enlightened one. Katya is lonely, loathed by her mother-in-law Kabanicha and no longer in love with her husband Tikhon. While her husband is away, Katya falls in love with Boris – the music is rapturous at this point. When her husband returns, Katya seemingly unhinged by guilt, confesses her adultery and Boris is exiled to Siberia. Katya drowns herself in the river.

The Love for Three Oranges (1921)

(Lyubov k trem Apelsinam)
Sergei Sergeyevich Prokofiev

I first saw this opera at the Teatro Communale in Florence where I earnestly read the libretto, which they gave out with the tickets. It was, of course, in Italian and I assumed my Italian was worse than I thought, as it seemed to be about a hypochondriac prince who falls in love with an orange. It turned out I was right. Prokofiev's absurdist opera opens in the court of the King of Clubs, who is looking for a cure for his melancholy son's illness, and is persuaded the only antidote is that he laughs. Though the jester tries his best, the only one who makes the Prince laugh is unfortunately the witch

Fata Morgana. Her revenge is that the Prince will fall in love with three oranges and pursue them to the ends of the earth. The action moves to the desert, where the Prince finds his three oranges. The first two open to reveal two princesses, but they die of thirst. When the third orange reveals a third princess, Ninetta – to whom the Prince is happy to devote the rest of his life – the on-stage "audience" in despair find a bucket of water so her life is saved. Fata Morgana tries to intervene again (turning Ninetta temporarily into a rat), but all ends happily with a wedding.

The Cunning Little Vixen (1924)

(Príhody Lisky Bystrousky)
Leos Janacek

Janacek's magic tale of humans and animals was based – most unusually! – on a series of newspaper articles that featured a half-tame vixen. A forester catches a young vixen to bring up as a pet but on the first night in his house she seems to metamorphose into a girl – perhaps it is the gypsy girl the forester dreams of, the embodiment of freedom? The vixen indeed wants her freedom and tries to provoke the other animals to revolt, but they are not interested, and she bites off the chickens' heads and escapes to the woods where she marries a fox. She is accidentally killed by a poacher (who is about to marry the gypsy girl of the forester's dreams). The forester is sad and returns to the wood where he found the little vixen. He sees one of her cubs playing and tries in vain to catch it, but is consoled at the sight of nature renewing herself.

Wozzeck (1925)

Alban Berg

Berg was a pupil of Schoenberg and, though influenced by his master, *Wozzeck* is not composed according to Schoenberg's dodecaphonic (twelve tone) method. The music is extremely compelling and finishes in an orchestral lament, full of compassion for humankind's sorry state. The story is taken from the play of the same name by Georg Buchner and tells of the simple-minded soldier Wozzeck, who is preyed upon by those around him. A mad doctor experiments on him, his Captain patronizes him, while his mistress Marie betrays him. As a result, Wozzeck cuts her throat, and, returning later to dispose of the knife, wades into the lake trying to wash away the blood and drowns. When the news of his mother's death is brought to Wozzeck and Marie's young child, he seems not to take it in, continuing to play on his hobby horse as the curtain falls.

DID YOU KNOW?
Berg became a pupil of Schoenberg because his brother, Charley, saw Schoenberg's advertisement for students and took his brother's songs for him to look at. Alban had just entered the civil service.

Turandot (1926)

Giacomo Puccini

It will always be remembered by the football-loving public around the world for Pavarotti's rendition of 'Nessum dorma', but Puccini's *Turandot* has far more going for it, sublime as that particular aria is. Turandot is the daughter of the Emperor of China, so famed for her beauty that suitors come from far away to claim her as a bride – and the throne of China. She tests them by asking three riddles. If they guess correctly, they win her hand; if not, the penalty is death. Blind, banished King Timur, guided by his faithful slave girl Liu, meet Calaf, Timur's son, whom he thought dead, but the joy is short lived as Calaf glimpses Turandot and, smitten, decides to submit to the test. His father and Liu, who loves Calaf, beg him not to do it and there is an exquisite musical moment for Liu. The three ministers of the Imperial Household, Ping, Pang and Pong, provide some comedy at the start of the second act, but the trial draws on, starting with Turandot's own telling of her family history and her desire to slake the thirst of an ancient desire for revenge – hence the trial of those who try to conquer her. Calaf answers the riddles correctly and Turandot pleads with the Emperor not to have to marry the foreign prince. Calaf offers her one last chance – if she can find out his name, he will accept death. Act III starts with 'Nessum dorma' – no one shall sleep while the Princess searches for the prince's name. Ping, Pang and Pong try bribes and threats but Calaf refuses to tell. Timur and Liu are captured and, protecting Timur, Liu says only she knows the name. She is tortured but refuses to tell, stabbing herself with a soldier's dagger. Calaf is angry with Turandot but, finally, kisses her and she is overcome. He tells her his name but when the Emperor comes Turandot does not want his life, but announces the stranger's name is 'Love'.

Aufstieg und Fall der Stadt Mahagonny (1930)

(The Rise and Fall of the City of Mahagonny)
Kurt Weill

Although perhaps better known for their collaboration on the musical *The Threepenny Opera*, Kurt Weill and Bertolt Brecht also wrote an opera, *Mahagonny*. Its premiere in Leipzig caused demonstrations by the Nazis, who banished the composer and author, banning their works. The opera is an anti-capitalist satire set in a mythical America where Jim Mahoney and his friends found a city – Mahagonny – devoted to pleasure. It is peopled by criminals, murderers and call girls and there is gluttony, lust, gambling and fighting galore. The worst crime in Mahagonny, though, is to run out of money, and Jim Mahoney is put on trial for this. The death penalty is given due to his failure to pay for whisky and he ends up in the electric chair.

Lady Macbeth of Mtsensk (1934)

(Katerina Ismailova)
Dmitri Dmitriyevich Shostakovich

Shostakovich's opera is a strange mixture of parody, tragedy and farce bundled together with an undeniable lyricism and moments of musical brilliance. Katerina is unhappily married to Zinovy, but her lecherous father-in-law Boris plans to seduce her. She takes the family's labourer, Sergei, as her lover instead and Boris beats him when he finds out. Katerina murders Boris with rat poison in revenge and then kills Zinovy. Katerina marries Sergei but Zinovy's body is discovered and the two are arrested and sent to prison camp, where Sergei abandons Katerina for Sonyetka, another inmate. Katerina attacks her and the two women drown in the river.

Porgy and Bess (1935)

George Gershwin

Gershwin's opera broke many taboos. It combined lush orchestration with spirituals and jazz; it played consecutive nights (not in rep like most operas); and it featured a story of the poor blacks of America's South, played by a company of black singers. It also features such songs as 'Summertime', 'It Ain't Necessarily So' and 'There's a Boat Leaving Soon'. Set in a tenement on Charleston's waterfront, it tells the story of the crippled Porgy's love for Bess and his rivalry with Crown that leads to Crown's death. Bess has been lured by drug dealer Sportin' Life's 'happy dust' to New York, believing she won't see Porgy again. Unexpectedly, Porgy is released from prison, and arriving back at the tenement vows to go to New York and find Bess.

Lulu (1937)

Alban Berg

Berg's second opera was written according to Schoenberg's dodecaphonic system and Schoenberg was asked to write the final act, Berg having died with only the first two completed. He refused and the opera was performed unfinished for many years until Friedrich Cerha – with much encouragement from Pierre Boulez – finally completed it in 1979, when Boulez conducted it. Lulu first appears dressed as Pierrot, having her portrait painted. The painter tries to seduce Lulu but they are interrupted as her husband arrives, immediately dying with shock at seeing the pair in a compromising position. This sets the tone for the rest of the story – Lulu is an amoral creature who destroys everyone who desires her. The next scene sees the painter now Lulu's new husband. However, she is also the lover of Dr Schön, who tells the painter that she has been known by a different name by each of her lovers. The painter commits suicide. She goes on to murder Schön, but escapes from prison with his son Alwa and they run away first to Paris and then to London, where Lulu works as a prostitute – one of her clients kills Alwa. Her last customer is Jack the Ripper, who murders Lulu and Grafin Geschwitz, Lulu's lesbian lover, who has come to her aid.

The Rake's Progress (1951)

Igor Federovich Stravinsky

Stravinsky's masterpiece is based on a text by WH Auden, based in turn on Hogarth's 'Rake's Progress' series of paintings. A cautionary moral tale, it tells of the downfall of Tom Rakewell, first seen courting Anne Trulove in her father's garden. He refuses her father's offer of work but, finding he has inherited a fortune, leaves Anne and heads for London. Under the tutelage of Nick Shadow, his downward spiral begins with brothels, drinking and profligacy, he is tricked into marrying Baba, the bearded lady, loses his fortune and ends up in the madhouse, Nick having been revealed as the Devil.

A Midsummer Night's Dream (1960)

Benjamin Britten

It is hard to decide on which Britten opera to include in a list such as this – *The Turn of the Screw*, *Billy Budd* and *Peter Grimes* are all regularly performed and enjoyed around the world. *A Midsummer Night's Dream* has, though, not only some of Britten's most inventive and evocative music, but it uses Shakespeare's play to great effect, shifting the focus strongly on to the fairies and a magic that does not always work in favour of the humans. Oberon is sung by a countertenor while Puck is a speaking role and the opera's plot closely follows that of the play: Oberon and Titania's quarrel, the quartet of lovers, the rude mechanicals (now with an opera rather than a play), and Titania's deluded love for one of them – Bottom, transformed into an ass.

Chapter 2

OPERA'S GREATEST COMPOSERS

Claudio Monteverdi (1567–1643)

The first great composer of what can truly be termed opera was without doubt Claudio Monteverdi. He was musically gifted as a child and had his first pieces published by a Venetian music publisher when he was just fifteen. In his twenties, he found a place in the court of Mantua as musician and composer, and eventually *maestro di cappella*. He singlehandedly transformed the fledgling art form of opera – known at the time as the 'new music', le *nuove musiche* – that was evolving at the end of the sixteenth century in Florence. It was based on a desire to return to the high art of the classical world (this was, after all, the Renaissance) and this was particularly evident in the subject matter of the early operas. The group who were most influential were known as the Camerata, and included composers such as Vincenzo Galilei (father of the astronomer), Emilio de' Cavalieri, Jacopo Peri and Giulio Caccini. While the music of the classical world was lost forever, they believed that the story and the words must be clear – a reaction against polyphony, where voices overlapped and meaning was often lost. So these composers decided to base their work on the *recitativo* or recitative, a single vocal line (monody) accompanied by supporting instrumental music. While the new art form gradually advanced, before Monteverdi the operas had been rather pedestrian. Monteverdi was to catapult the New Music into an altogether higher sphere. His first opera, *Orfeo*, accepted all of the current theories but charged them with drama and musical brilliance. Dismissed from his post when the old Duke of Mantua died – despite being the most famous composer in Europe at the time – Monteverdi became the *maestro di cappella* at St Mark's in Venice and eventually took holy orders and became a priest. Of the twenty-one music-dramas he composed, only seven survive, and of those some are mere fragments. However, they are more than enough to demonstrate he was opera's first musical genius. *La Favola d'Orfeo* (*The Legend of Orpheus*) and *L'Incoronazione di Poppea* (*The Coronation of Poppea*) – the latter written at the age of seventy-five – are the most popular and widely performed of his operas today.

DID YOU KNOW?

In August 1613, on his way to take up his post of *maestro di cappella* at St Mark's in Venice, Monteverdi was set upon and robbed by two highwaymen.

Pietro Francesco Cavalli (1602–1676)

Cavalli was the son of Battista Caletti Bruni, the *maestro di cappella* at the cathedral of Crema in northern Italy, but he took his name from the town's governor, Federigo Cavalli, who sent him to Venice to study. He became a singer at St Mark's in Venice at the age of fourteen and as a young man became a renowned singer in the city. In 1637 he wrote his first opera, *Le Nozze di Teti e di Peleo*, and he became an equally renowned composer. More operas (he wrote forty-two in all) followed, including *Orione*, *L'Ormindo*, *La Calisto*, *L'Ercole Amante*, *Serse*, *Scipione Africano*, *Mutio Scevol* and *Pompeo Magno*. There has been a revival of interest in Cavalli with performances and recordings of his operas over recent decades.

Jean-Baptiste Lully (1632–1687)

Though he was born in obscurity, the son of a miller in Florence, Lully was to become the founding father of French opera, the richest composer of the day and a friend of Louis XIV. He became *valet de chambre* at the age of fourteen to a French noblewoman, Mlle de Montpensier, and at the age of twenty went to Paris and the court where he was a noted musician and dancer, appearing in the *Ballet de la nuit*. King Louis XIV made him *compositeur de la musique instrumentale*. Lully wrote the music for numerous successful court *comedies-ballets* and in 1661 he took French nationality. He noticed, too, that the tide was turning in favour of more serious musical productions and he created *Cadmus et Hermione* in 1673, which drew together ballet and the new Italian opera. More followed in rapid succession, including *Alceste, Thésée, Atys, Isis, Psyché, Bellérophon, Prosperine, Persée, Phaéton, Amadis, Roland* and *Armide*.

DID YOU KNOW?
Lully was famed as a libertine, even by the standards of the court of Louis XIV. He had affairs with men and women and was continually in the midst of a scandal, but Louis always forgave him as he was essential for the king's musical entertainment.

Henry Purcell (1658/1659–1695)

Henry Purcell was the first English composer of operas and the composer of the first opera to be written in English. This was *Dido and Aeneas* and was, perhaps rather surprisingly, performed by the young ladies of Mr Josias Priest's school in Chelsea. It is only an hour in length and many of the details of that first performance (including Purcell's autograph copy of the score) have been lost, but there is no dispute that this is a beautiful piece, with Dido's lament a poignant and masterful aria. As a child, Purcell was a chorister at the Chapel Royal and he became 'composer in ordinary' there at eighteen or nineteen. Much of his music was religious, including anthems and other pieces for services. But he wrote plenty of secular music too, including songs, sonatas for strings and keyboards, and pieces for organ and harpsichord. Purcell also went on to write music for the stage – *King Arthur* and *The Fairy Queen*, for instance – but these were not operas in the true sense, more incidental music for plays and masques. But these and his songs were all quite beautiful, and had he not died so young one can only wonder at what else he might have created for the world of opera.

A WORTHY COMPOSER

On his death, aged just thirty-six, *The Flying Post* newspaper wrote:

Mr Henry Pursel [sic] one of the most celebrated Masters of the Science of Musick in the kingdom and scare inferiour to any in Europe, dying on Thursday last; the Dean of Westminster, knowing the great worth of the deceased, forthwith summoned a Chapter, and unanimously resolved that he shall be interred in the Abbey, with all the Funeral Solemnity they are capable to perform for him, granting his widow the choice of the ground to reposit his Corps free from any charge, who has appointed it at the foot of the Organs, and this evening he will be interred, the whole Chapter assisting with their vestments; together with all the Lovers of that Noble Science, with the united Choyres of that and the Chappel Royal, when the Dirge composed by the Deceased for her late Majesty of Ever Blessed Memory, will be Played by Trumpets and other Musick.

Alessandro Scarlatti (1660–1725)

Alessandro was the father of the more famous Domenico Scarlatti but he was also a considerable composer of operas in his own right. His first opera, *Gli euivoci nel sembiante*, was produced when he was just nineteen at the Teatro Capranica in Rome and was watched by Queen Christina of Sweden, who made him her *maestro di cappella*. His second opera, *L'honestà negli amori*, soon followed. His next opera in 1683, *Psiche*, saw him also made *maestro di cappella* at the royal palace in Naples. He travelled to Rome with his son Domenico where Cardinal Ottoboni became his patron and in 1707 he wrote two operas there, *Mitridate Eupatore* and *Il trionfo della libertà*. More operas followed, noted for their fluency and expressiveness, including *Tigrone*, *Carlo, re d'Alemagna*, *Telemaco*, *Marco Attilo Regolo* and *Griselda*.

DID YOU KNOW?
Alessandro's other son, Pietro Filippo Scarlatti, was also a composer.

Antonio Lucio Vivaldi (1678–1741)

While the Baroque composer Vivaldi is best known today for his instrumental music, including the phenomenally enduring *The Four Seasons*, he was also a prolific composer of operas, producing according to his own calculations almost a hundred, of which almost half survive to some extent. His father was a violinist and presumably gave him some early lessons, though little is known of this period of Vivaldi's life. At the age of fifteen he began training for the priesthood and became a priest. He was known as '*il prete rosso*' or 'the red priest', for his calling and his red hair. He taught music to the foundlings at Venice's Ospedale della Pietà and they performed his compositions, drawing large audiences. His first opera was *Ottone in villa* in 1713 and in each of the following fifteen years he would produce at least one new opera if not several. These included *Orlando finto pazzo*, *Nerone fatto Cesare*, *L'incoronazione di Dario*, *La costanza trionfante degli amori e degli odi* (later re-edited and entitled *Artabano re dei Parti*) and, in later years, *Farnace*, *L'Olimpiade*, *Catone in Utica* and *La Griselda*.

VIVALDI'S LOST TREASURES
Vivaldi's work was mostly forgotten until the early twentieth century, by which time much of it was lost. However, there have been some remarkable rediscoveries. Between 1926 and 1930 fourteen folios were found in the library of a monastery in Piedmont and with the descendants of the Grand Duke Durazzo. Between them, these amounted to 300 concertos and 18 operas. Discoveries have continued, the most recent being in 2006 when the harpsichordist and conductor Ondrej Macek found Vivaldi's 1730 opera *Argippo*, which he performed with the Hofmusici orchestra at Prague Castle, its first performance since the year of its composition.

Jean-Philippe Rameau (1683–1764)

Rameau was both a composer and a music theorist, taking over from Lully as the chief composer of French opera and writing his *Treatise on Harmony* in 1722. It was not until his fifties, however, that he started writing opera, having previously written mostly harpsichord pieces and cantatas. His first opera, *Hippolyte et Aricie*, was written with the Abbé Pellegrin as his librettist. It provoked much controversy – some seeing his harmonic innovations as undermining French musical traditions – but it was generally acknowledged as the best French opera since Lully. Rameau's operas were also often ballets, such as *La Princesse de Navarre*, *Platée* and *Les Indes galantes*. His tragic operas include *Castor et Polux*, *Dardanus* and *Zoroastre*. While his music has been neglected for a long time, it has recently been rediscovered in performance & recordings.

DID YOU KNOW?

Rameau and the philosopher Jean-Jacques Rousseau were bitter enemies. Rousseau had pretensions as a composer and Rameau and Voltaire commissioned him to turn Rameau's *comedie-ballet La Princesses de Navarre* into an opera with linking recitative. Rousseau claimed they stole the credit for his work – though musicologists can find little trace of it – and his resentment was to explode a few years later in the *Querelle des Bouffons*. Rousseau caricatured Rameau's music as out of date, comparing it unfavourably with the new Italian *opera buffa*.

George Frideric Handel (1685–1759)

Handel is a towering figure in the history of opera and, though forgotten until a few decades ago, he is now widely performed. Though born in Germany and trained there and in Italy, he lived for most of his productive life in London, arriving there in late 1710. His first work for the stage was *Rinaldo*, which he wrote in a fortnight, and was a major success when it was performed at the Queen's Theatre in the Haymarket. Handel wrote music at an extraordinary speed, *The Messiah*, for instance, in little more than three weeks, and when under pressure would often leave gaps in organ concertos to be filled in by improvisation on the spot. He wrote more than forty operas, as well as many other works, notably his oratorios (such as *The Messiah*) and music for specific occasions (*Water Music*, *Musick for the Royal Fireworks*). Handel obeyed the conventions of the day – heroes were sung by *castrati* (now these parts are often taken by female mezzo-sopranos); the music was dominated by the solo aria, after which the singer would leave the stage, so there was little interaction; there were almost no ensembles and no chorus. Even within this restrictive genre, Handel wrote music that was dramatic and characters who were fully drawn. Some of his most popular operas include *Rinaldo*, *Acis and Galatea* (composed to a libretto by John Gay), *Giulio Cesare*, *Tamerlano*, *Ariodante*, *Alcina*, *Xerxes* and *Semele*.

Cardinal Ottoboni arranged a musical contest at one of his *Academie Poetico Muiscali* in Rome between Scarlatti and Handel. John Mainwaring tells the story thus:

When it came to the organ there was not the least pretence for doubting to which of them it belonged. Scarlatti himself declared the superiority of his antagonist, and owned ingenuously, that till he had heard him upon this instrument, he had no conception of its powers. Handel used often to speak of [Scarlatti] with great satisfaction and indeed there was reason for it; for besides his great talent as an artist he had the sweetest temper and the genteelest behaviour. On the other hand, it was mentioned that Scarlatti as oft as he was admired for his great execution would mention Handel and cross himself in veneration.

Domenico Scarlatti (1685–1757)

Born into the intensely musical household of his father Alessandro Scarlatti, Domenico became organist and composer of the royal chapel in Naples under the watchful eye of his father in 1701. He wrote his first opera, *Ottavia risituta al trono*, produced at the Teatro San Bartolomeo, when he was just eighteen. Two more operas followed within a year, *Giustina* and *Irene*. In 1709, Scarlatti entered the service of Maria Casimira, Queen of Poland, and wrote several operas including *La Sylvia*, *Orland*, *Tolomeo e Alessandro* and *Amor d'un ombra*. As *maestro di cappella* at the Cappella Giuliana he was also a prolific composer of church music, including two Misereres and a ten-part Stabat Mater. Scarlatti is best remembered today for his harpsichord music.

A SPIRITUAL COMPOSER

Chopin in his role as piano teacher thought highly of Scarlatti, writing:

Those of my dear colleagues who teach the piano are unhappy that I make my own pupils work on Scarlatti. But I am surprised that they are so blinkered. His music contains finger-exercises aplenty and more than a touch of the most elevated spirituality. Sometimes he is even a match for Mozart. If I were not afraid of incurring the disapprobation of numerous fools, I would play Scarlatti at my concerts. I maintain that the day will come when Scarlatti's music will often be played at concerts and that audiences will appreciate and enjoy it.

A VIRTUOSO COMPOSER

Dr Charles Burney's *History of Music*, published between 1776 and 1789, recalls (an acquaintance) Roseingrave's report of meeting the young Domenico Scarlatti thus:

Being arrived in Venice in his way to Rome, as he himself told me, he was invited, as a stranger and a virtuoso, to an academia at the house of a nobleman, where, among others, he was requested to sit down to the harpsichord and favour the company with a toccata, as a specimen *della sua virtù*. And, says he 'finding myself rather better in courage and finger than usual, I exerted myself and fancied by the applause I received, that my performance had made some impression on the company. After a cantata had been sung by a scholar of Fr Gasparini, who was there to accompany her, a grave young man dressed in black and in a black wig, who had stood in one corner of the room, very quiet and attentive while Roseingrave played, being asked to sit down to the harpsichord, when he began to play, Rosy said, he thought that ten hundred demons had been at the instrument; he never had heard such passages of execution and effect before. The performance so far surpassed his own, and every degree of perfection to which he thought it possible he should ever arrive that, if he had been in sight of any instrument with which to have done the deed, he would have cut off his own fingers. Upon enquiring the name of this extraordinary performer, was told it was Domenico Scarlatti, son of the celebrated Cavalier Alessandro Scarlatti.

John Gay (1685–1732)

Gay is best known for *The Beggar's Opera* of 1728. The music is drawn from a variety of sources, including contemporary ballads, folk songs and other operas of the day. A political and social satire, it dealt with low life and corruption, and its sequel, *Polly*, was banned during Gay's own lifetime. *The Beggar's Opera* was a runaway success and even threatened Handel's supreme position and the genre of *opera seria*. Gay was also the librettist of Handel's *Acis and Galatea* and was responsible for the building of the first Covent Garden Theatre in 1732.

Thomas Arne (1710–1778)

Thomas Arne was born in London, in King Street in Covent Garden. His first opera, *Rosamund*, appeared at the Lincoln's Inn Fields Theatre in 1733 with his sister, Susannah, in the title role and his younger brother, Michael, as the page. He was very attracted by the idea of the masque and produced several. In 1744 he became resident composer at the Theatre, Drury Lane and wrote three comic operas, all appearing there in 1745 – *The Temple of Dullness*, *The Picture* and *King Pepin's Campaign*. In 1760 he met the librettist Isaac Bickerstaff and a productive collaboration followed, with *Thomas and Sally*, *Judith* and *Love in a Village*. These were all comic operas, but he also composed an *opera seria* for Covent Garden – 1762's *Artaxerxes* – that had considerable success. He wrote several more comic operas including *The Guardian Outwitted*, *The Cooper*, *The Rose* and *Achilles in Petticoats*, which enjoyed success at the time, though his operas are rarely performed today.

THE SECRET COMPOSER

Arne's musical ambitions were not encouraged by his family when he was a child. His pupil Dr Charles Burney, who was also the author of a *History of Music* (1782–1789), recalled his secret studies:

He used to avail himself of the privilege of a servant, by borrowing livery and going into the upper gallery of the opera, which was then appropriated to domestics. At home he had contrived to secrete a spinet in his room, upon which, after muffling the strings with a handkerchief, he used to practise in the night while the rest of the family were asleep.

Christoph Willibald Gluck (1714–1787)

Brought up in what is the modern-day Czech Republic, Gluck went to the University of Prague where he earned money by teaching and performing on the violin, cello and keyboard instruments. In 1736 he secured a position as a chamber musician in the household of Prince Lobkowitz in Vienna and went on to work in Milan, Venice, Bologna, Crema, Turin, London – and just about every city in Europe. Gluck was one of opera's great reformers. He began his composing life with the florid *opera seria* beloved of Handel and virtually all of the other composers of the day but became convinced that the genre was an obstacle to the drama and that this should be more important than ballets, sets and even music, though Gluck's music is undeniably beautiful. He strove for simplicity and accomplished it in his first 'reformed' opera, *Orfeo ed Euridice*. In this opera and those that followed, he turned his back on the vocal virtuosity of the solo singer in favour of harmony, orchestration and dramatic purpose. It is sometimes argued that in this respect Gluck was an early precursor of Wagner. Certainly, his reforms aroused huge controversy in their day – even duels were fought over the relative merits of the two musical forms! He became the Grand Old Man of music in his later years and gave support to younger composers such as Mozart and, especially, Salieri. Gluck continued with his new style and he went on to write *Alceste*, *Iphigenie en Aulide*, *Armide*, *Iphigenie en Tauride* and *Echo et Narcisse* among many others.

DID YOU KNOW?
After his opera *Antigone* was produced in Rome in 1756, Pope Benedict XIV made Gluck a Knight of the Golden Spur.

Johann Christian Bach (1735–1782)

Johann Christian was the youngest son of Johann Sebastian Bach and he was taught first by his father and then his half-brother, Carl Philipp Emanuel. He travelled to Italy in the 1750s and there became much enamoured of opera, though he was also writing church music at the time. His first Italian opera, *Artasere*, was produced at Turin in 1761 and *Catone in Utica* appeared later that year in Naples, *Alesandro nell'Indie* the following year. That same year he went to London to compose an opera,

Orione ossia Diana Vendicata, which was an immediate success. He became music master to Queen Charlotte, wife of George III, and while in London also composed chamber music and gained a great reputation as a performer of his own and other composers' music. More operas appeared, too, for the London stage – *Zanaida*, *Adriano in Siria* and *Carattaco*. His final London opera was *La Clemenza di Scipione* in 1778 and later that year he wrote *Amadis des Gaules* for the Paris opera, though it was not a major success. He returned to London but never managed to regain his former standing – and hence paying pupils – and died leaving considerable debts.

DID YOU KNOW?

Johann Christian Bach was known as 'the English Bach' because he spent so much time in the country. He was also the first notable performer to introduce audiences to the piano – a concert in St James's Street, London, in 1768 had 'a Solo on the Piano Forte by Mr Bach'.

Carl Ditters von Dittersdorf (1739–1799)

August Carl Ditters began playing the violin at the age of six and, by age eleven, he had obtained a post with the Viennese Schottenkircheorchestra. He met both Gluck and Haydn and became court composer to the Prince-Bishop of Breslau, where he remained for twenty years performing and writing symphonies, chamber music and comic opera. He was ennobled in 1773, becoming Carl Ditters von Dittersdorf. His operas include *Amore in Musica*, *Doktor und Apotheker*, *Die Liebe im Narrenhaus*, *Hieronymus Knicker*, *Das Gespent mit der Tromme* and *Don Quixote der Zweyte*.

Giovanni Paisiello (1740–1816)

Though rarely heard today, in his own lifetime Paisiello was a star composer, particularly in the *opera buffa* vein. His works included *Il re*

Teodoro, *Pirro*, *Nina*, *La Molinara* and, most famously, *Il Barbiere di Siviglia* in 1782, one of three versions of Beaumarchais' play, which only gradually lost its pre-eminence to Rossini's, written in 1816.

André Grétry (1741–1813)

Beginning his musical education as a somewhat reluctant and unsuccessful choirboy in Liège, Grétry started to produce compositions that were good enough to win him a grant to study in Rome. He went to Geneva where he met Voltaire, who encouraged him to go to Paris. On arrival, after a few failures, he wrote a comic opera, *Le Huron*, that was an immediate hit and the first of some fifty operas including *Le Huron*, *Andromaque*, *Lucile*, *Le Tableau parlant*, *Les deux avares*, *Sylvain*, *Zémire et Azor*, *Le magnifique*, *Le jugement de Midas*, *Aucassin et Nicolette*, *Colinette à la cour*, *La Caravane du Caire*, *Richard Coeur-de-lion*, *Pierre le Grand*, *Guillaume Tell* and *La casque et les colombes*.

Domenico Cimarosa (1749–1801)

Cimarosa was an opera composer of the Neapolitan school, writing over eighty mostly *opera buffa*s during his lifetime. His first came at the age of twenty-three, *Le stravaganze del conte*, and for the next few years he toured Italy conducting and writing operas. In 1788 Empress Catherine II invited him to St Petersburg where he worked and composed for four years before accepting the position of *Kapellmeister* from Leopold II in Vienna. Here he produced his masterpiece, *Il matrimonio segreto* – a triumph from its premiere at the Burgtheater in Vienna. After Leopold's death he returned to Naples where *Il matrimonio segreto* repeated its success, and wrote many more operas, the comic ones always more successful than the serious ones. His works included *L'Amida immaginaria*, *L'Italiana in Londra*, *Le donne rivali*, *Giannina e Bernardone*, *La ballerina amante*, *Il vecchio burlato*, *Artaserse*, *L'impresario in angustie*, *Il maestro di cappella* and *L'astuzie femminili*.

DID YOU KNOW?
Emperor Leopold II was so entranced by *Il matrimonio segreto* that he gave the cast supper – and then made them sing the opera again.

Antonio Salieri (1750–1825)

Mostly known nowadays as Mozart's great rival (and perhaps murderer) in the play and film *Amadeus*, Salieri was a highly regarded composer in his day. Peter Schaffer's play was not, though, the first to suggest a dark history between the two composers. Within a few months of Salieri's death, Aleksandr Pushkin wrote *Mozart and Salieri*, and it was later turned into an opera by Rimsky-Korsakov. Salieri worked mostly in the royal court of Vienna and taught Beethoven and Schubert. He wrote more than forty operas, including *Les Danaïdes*, *Falsaff* and *Tarare*, and these, together with a few of his other operas and arias taken from them, are gradually making their way into the opera house, concert hall and recordings.

Wolfgang Amadeus Mozart (1756–1791)

Mozart is without peer in the pantheon of composers. He took not only the best of Handel's *opera seria* and Gluck's sense of drama and harmony, but *opera buffa*, itself with links back to *commedia dell'arte*, and the developing orchestral and symphonic forms. From all of these, forged together with a true genius, he produced in a startlingly short time works that are still favourites in opera houses all over the world. A child prodigy, he toured the courts of Europe from an early age, performing for emperors and princes. His older sister, Nannerl, would recall later: 'He learned a piece in an hour, and a minuet in half an hour, so that he could play it faultlessly and with the greatest delicacy, and keeping exactly in time. He made such progress that by the age of five he was already composing little pieces.' Mozart's childhood was a gruelling round of European cities and royal courts devised by his musician father, Leopold Mozart. He had a troubled relationship with most of his employers, being literally kicked out of the service of the Archbishop of Salzburg by his steward. After his marriage to Constanze Weber, he tried to make a living by composing and teaching, but it was always a struggle for survival and there was never enough money for the young couple to live on comfortably. Mozart hoped for a court position in Vienna – and hoped on. His work was often greeted with enthusiastic success but financially he always on the back foot, though in his later years he was composing at an extraordinary rate. He did eventually receive a court appointment as Composer to the Emperor in Vienna, but his salary was nominal and Mozart was to end his life in poverty, buried in a pauper's grave. His first opera, *La Finta Semplice*, was written when he was just twelve. He wrote several other operas while he was a teenager, including the *opera seria Mitridate, Rè di Ponto* and the comic opera *La Finta Giardiniera*. He was to write two more *operas serias* in later years – *Idomeneo* and *La Clemenza di Tito*. But he wrote comic operas, too, such as *Die Entführung aus dem Serail* (*The Escape from the Seraglio*, 1782). And it was with the librettist Lorenzo Da Ponte that he wrote a trio of masterpieces – *Le Nozze di Figaro* (1786), *Don Giovanni* (1787) and *Così Fan Tutte* (1790). In the last year of his life he wrote *Die Zauberflöte* (*The Magic Flute*), *La Clemenza di Tito* and his great Requiem. In Mozart, one finds wit and charm, humanity and morality and above all sublime music. It is hardly surprising he is such a staple of the repertoire today.

DID YOU KNOW?

In Rome, Mozart heard Gregorio Allegri's sublime Miserere sung in the Sistine Chapel. The Vatican, determined to keep this treasure to itself, banned the publication of the music. Mozart went home and wrote it out note for note with only the tiniest of errors. He was thirteen years old.

Luigi Cherubini (1760–1842)

Cherubini was born in Florence and studied in Venice with Giuseppe Sarti. He wrote his first opera, *Quinto Fabio*, in 1780. This was followed in 1783 by *Lo Sposo di tre, Marito di Nessuna, Idalide* and *Alessandro nelle Indie*. He wrote two more operas in London, then went to Paris and back to Italy, where he produced *Didone abbandonata* and *Ifigenia in Aulide*. He returned to Paris in 1788 and stayed there for the rest of his life, adapting remarkably to the revolutionary times and writing *Lodokiska*, set in Poland, and *Les Deux Journées*, with a peasant hero. Beethoven regarded him as the greatest living composer of the time.

DID YOU KNOW?

The Theatre de Monsieur where Cherubini conducted an Italian repertoire from 1789 to 1792 was set up by one Léonard, hairdresser to Marie Antoinette.

Ludwig van Beethoven (1770–1827)

Beethoven's childhood was, frankly, squalid. His father, a feckless alcoholic, did actually serve as a musician in the chapel of the Elector in Bonn, as had Beethoven's grandfather before him. The composer was one of seven children, of whom only he and two younger brothers survived, and despite his obvious talent in music he received little general education. He did, though, learn the pianoforte, organ, violin and viola and was so prodigious he became the court organist's assistant in 1784. By the age of nineteen, his father having been dismissed from his post, Beethoven was the family's sole earner. As a young man, he moved to Vienna, and was fortunate to find patrons who recognized his brilliance. He was, after all, one of the greatest composers of all time and produced a wealth of piano and violin sonatas, string quartets and symphonies. Beethoven wrote only one opera, *Fidelio*. It was commissioned by Schikaneder, the librettist and producer of Mozart's *Magic Flute*, and the story (taken from a French book by Bouilly) had already been used by three other composers. The opera itself had many flaws and flopped when it was first performed. Beethoven – who was passionate about his subject matter – made several revisions and it finally became a success in 1814, nine years after the first version was seen. Now it is regarded as one of the great German operas. It is set within the *Singspiel* tradition but defies narrow categorization and is a moving tribute to love, liberty and the human spirit. Beethoven did consider other operatic subjects, but *Fidelio* was the only one he ever completed.

François Adrien Boïeldieu (1775–1834)

Though little performed today, Boïeldieu was not only an enormous success as an opera composer in the late eighteenth century, but he virtually defined the *opera comique* for all time. Success came early to him, too. He wrote his first, *La Fille Coupable*, to a libretto by his father and it was performed in his home town of Rouen. A second local success persuaded the young composer to go to Paris, where he staged *La Famille Suisse*, again winning instant approval. He spent eight years in St Petersburg as conductor of the Imperial Opera and continued writing operas. On his return to Paris in 1812, his new opera, *Jean de Paris*, was greeted rapturously by audiences. His finest opera is generally accepted to be *La Dame Blanche*, based on two novels by Sir Walter Scott, with a libretto by Eugène Scribe. It is occasionally performed today, most recently in the Salle Favart in Paris in 1997.

> **DID YOU KNOW?**
> His early opera *Le Calife de Bagdad* was a huge popular hit, though Cherubini remarked to him at the theatre, 'Aren't you ashamed of such ill-deserved success?' Boïeldieu's response was to ask humbly for Cherubini's tuition.

Daniel Auber (1782–1871)

Though Daniel Auber was a master of the *opera comique*, his first foray into that world, *Le Séjour militaire* in 1813, was a failure and he wrote nothing until 1819 when *Le Testament et les billets-doux* appeared – and was another failure. Two years later, however, he was rewarded by success in the shape of *La Bergère Châtelaine*. In all he wrote almost fifty operas, often with Eugène Scribe as his librettist. He became Director of the Paris Conservatoire in 1842 and Napoleon III made him 'maître de chapelle'. Some of his most famous works were *Le Cheval de bronze*, *Le Domino noir* and *Les Diamants de la Couronne*, but they are little played today, though the overtures sometimes are – they are as brilliant and vivacious as those of Rossini.

DID YOU KNOW?
Auber was such a shy man he never attended the performances of any of his own compositions.

Gasparo Spontini (1774–1851)

Born in Italy, Spontini spent most of his working life in Paris and Berlin, where he became a celebrated composer and conductor of operas, though he is little known today. His first success was *Li Puntigli delle donner* in 1796 and his many other operas include *L'eroismo ridicolo*, *La fuga in maschera*, *La Petite Maison*, *Julie*, *La Vestale*, *Fernand Cortez*, *Olympie*, *Pélage, ou le Roi de la Paix*, *Nurmahal*, *Alcidor* and *Agnese von Hohenstaufen*. His first revival after many years was *La Vestale* at La Scala with Maria Callas in 1954 and there have been a few revivals of this and *Agnese von Hohenstaufen* over the following decades.

DID YOU KNOW?
From 1820, Spontini worked at the Prussian court of King Frederick William III, who much admired his music. However, with the rise of nationalism in German music, he fell from public favour and was hissed out of the theatre where he was conducting Mozart's *Don Giovanni*, the opera being abandoned for the night.

Carl Maria von Weber (1786–1826)

Weber is widely credited as the founding father of the Romantic movement and his influence can be seen in everyone from Wagner to Liszt and Chopin. Being born with a congenital disease of the hip, the young Carl Maria developed slowly physically but, in contrast, his father trained him in music so that he became known as a child performer and soon a composer too, his first compositions published when he was just eleven. In 1798 – aged twelve! – he wrote his first opera, *Die Macht der Liebe und des Weins* (*The Power of Love and Wine*), and his second was staged two years later, *Das stumme Waldmädchen* (*The Silent Forest Maiden*), though this has now been lost. He studied with Michael Haydn, brother of Joseph, in Salzburg and in Vienna with Abbé Vogler. His 1803 opera *Peter Schmoll und seine Nachbarn* (*Peter Schmoll and his Neighbours*) brought him his first popular success. While writing religious music alongside chamber and orchestral works, he focused on founding a new German form of opera in opposition to the Italian model that prevailed throughout Europe. Three successful operas came out during the following decade: *Silvana*, *Abu Hassan* (based on an *Arabian Nights* tale) and *Der Freischütz*, in which Weber finally found the soul of German romanticism, full of simple characters battling against the forces of nature and the supernatural. It remains his masterpiece, written just five years before his death, aged just forty, of consumption. He wrote three operas in the years left to him; one, *Die drei Pintos* (*The Three Pintos*), was unfinished on his death and the other two, *Euryanthe* and *Oberon*, both had magnificent music but such tortuous librettos that they are difficult to stage, though they have appeared more frequently recently and their overtures are still in the orchestral repertoire.

> **DID YOU KNOW?**
> Weber's cousin Constanze became the wife of Mozart.

Giacomo Meyerbeer (1791–1864)

Giacomo Meyerbeer was born Jakob Beer in Berlin, the son of a wealthy Jewish banker, but he was to find his greatest success in Paris as a composer of operas on the grandest of scales. His first operas, *Jephtha's Vow* and *Host and Guest* (also known as *The Two Caliphs* and *Alimek*), appeared in Germany but, on travelling to Italy in 1816, he fell under the spell of Rossini and took on a decidedly Italian manner thereafter. The operas that followed, including *The Crusader in Egypt* and *Emma di Resburgo*, were huge popular hits and Meyerbeer arrived in Paris in 1825 on the crest of a wave. Here he met Eugène Scribe, librettist to many successful composers of the day, and the two teamed up to produce *Robert le Diable*, *Les Huguenots*, *Le Prophète* and *L'Africaine*. All played to the growing love of spectacle and featured between them huge crowd scenes, ballets featuring everything from nuns to skaters, massacres, explosions and coronations.

> **DID YOU KNOW?**
> For the staging of his operas in Paris, Meyerbeer spent a great deal of his own money on scenery and, for the lighting, using Louis Daguerre, inventor of the daguerrotype.

Gioacchino Rossini (1792–1868)

Rossini created numerous operas in his long life, though he stopped composing at just thirty-seven. But then he began very early, and was much in demand on the piano, viola, horn and as a boy soprano. He trained at the Liceo Musicale in Bologna and by the time he left, when he was eighteen, he had already composed a great. He was hugely feted in the first half of the nineteenth century and composed comic, tragic and the newly popular historical (often with British subjects) operas. He wrote a well-received *opera seria*, *Tancredi*, based on the tragedy by Voltaire, then three months later, when he was only twenty-one, had his first highly acclaimed success, *L'Italiana in Algeri* (*The Italian Girl in Algiers*), written in just twenty-seven days in 1813. It is bursting with comic invention and high spirits and it was precisely these qualities that were to make Rossini popular to this day. *Elisabetta, Regina d'Inglaterra* followed and then his comic masterpiece, *Il Barbiere di Siviglia*, written in under two weeks. Based on the Beaumarchais play, it was the prequel to Mozart's earlier *Marriage of Figaro*. Works followed in rapid succession: *Otello*, *La Cenerentola* (*Cinderella*), *Mosè in Egitto* (*Moses in Egypt*), *La Donna del Lago* (*The Lady of the Lake*), *La Gazza Ladra* (*The Thieving Magpie*), *Semiramide*, *Le Comte Ory* and his final opera – which he believed his masterpiece – *Guillaume Tell* (*William Tell*). He died aged seventy-six, having written hardly any music at all for the second half of his life, but famed for the sparkling, witty operas of his youth.

Gaetano Donizetti (1797–1848)

Donizetti was – with Bellini and Rossini – part of the triumvirate that ruled Italian opera in the first half of the nineteenth century. Like Rossini, Donizetti composed rapidly and brilliant melodies poured out of him with ease. Aclaimed for his comedies, *L'Elisir d'Amore* (*The Elixir of Love*), *La Fille du Régiment* (*The Daughter of the Regiment*) and *Don Pasquale*, he composed equally fine tragic opera, notably *Lucia di Lammermoor*, *Lucrezia Borgia*, *Maria Stuarda* and *Anna Bolena*. In all, he composed almost seventy operas, but was generally neglected until re-discovered in the middle of the last century by dramatic sopranos such as Maria Callas and Dame Joan Sutherland, who recreated his fine coloratura roles.

DID YOU KNOW?
For many years there was a widely held belief that Donizetti was Scottish, his grandfather being a soldier called Donald Izett. There is no truth in the story.

was born into a theatrical family and married an actress, and he spent much of his time as an actor, a singer and an orchestral musician, playing the cello. He produced fourteen operas and eleven children. His first opera, in 1824, was *Ali Pascha von Janina*, but it was not a success – something he did not meet until his fourth, *Zar und Zimmerman*, which premiered in Leipzig in 1837, a story of Peter the Great and mistaken identities. It is still performed in Germany. His other operas include *Undine*, *Der Wildschütz* (*The Poacher*) and *Regina*, a revolutionary opera.

Vincenzo Bellini (1801–1835)

Though his father was the organist in Catania in Sicily, Bellini faced fierce opposition against his hope for a musical career. However, a Sicilian nobleman offered to fund his study at the Real Conservatorio di Musica in Naples, and it was here that the young Bellini wrote his first opera, *Adelson e Salvini*. He was invited to write *Il Pirata* for La Scala in Milan and this was to establish his name and demonstrate his flair for beautiful melodic lines – some musicologists believe their length and grace are due to the influence of Chopin. Though he was a follower of Rossini during his early years, Bellini is known less for sparkling comedies than for sublime outpourings of emotion, and is regarded by many as the precursor of Verdi and Puccini in his use of drama and character. He was not adverse to virtuosity and there are some stunning arias in his operas for the best coloratura sopranos – Bellini wrote some exceptional roles for women. His most popular works include *Norma*, *La Sonnambula* (*The Sleepwalker*) and *I Puritani* (*The Puritans*). He died aged just thirty-three.

Adolphe Adam (1803–1856)

Nowadays, Adolphe Adam is best known for his ballet score for *Giselle*, undoubtedly one of the most popular classical ballets still in the repertoire. In his own lifetime, however, he was best known as a composer of operas, in particular comic operas. His teacher, the composer Boïeldieu, was a master of the genre and he allowed the young Adam to compose the overture for his opera of 1825, *La Dame Blanche*. Adam's own first opera, *Pierre et Catherine*, was produced at the Opéra-Comique Theatre in Paris in 1829. There followed a string of operas that were very successful, given Adam's ability to write memorable melodies and orchestration. Some of the most popular comic operas were *Danilowa* and *Le Postilion de Longjumeau*. He did try his hand at grand opera – *Richard en Palestine* for instance – but these were never a success. He was the founder in 1847 of the Théâtre National in Paris as a venue for the works of new composers.

Hector Berlioz (1803–1869)

Perhaps better known for his orchestral music, Berlioz himself was always determined to write opera – a form he regarded as hugely important for any composer. Unfortunately, in his own lifetime, only one of his operas was ever actually performed in its entirety and even that was regarded at the time as a failure. This was the story of the artist, *Benvenuto Cellini*, performed at the Paris Opéra in 1838. This was followed by *La Damnation de Faust*, based like Gounod's version on Goethe, and the oratorio *L'Enfance du Christ*. His greatest opera, *Les Troyens* (*The Trojans*), was composed on so massive a scale, it could only be staged over two evenings. Berlioz only ever saw the first half, under the title *La Prise de Troie* (*The Capture of Troy*), performed and the first performance of the complete opera without any cuts was at Covent Garden in 1969! His final opera was based on Shakespeare's *Much Ado about Nothing* – *Béatrice et Bénédict*.

DID YOU KNOW?

Berlioz's most popular work, *Symphonie Fantastique*, centred around his amorous obsession with the English actress Harriet Smithson. The music was violently romantic and featured demons and witchcraft. It was, declared Berlioz, 'entirely autobiographical in intention'.

Mikhail Ivanovich Glinka (1804–1857)

Glinka has often been called the 'father of Russian music' and was an enormous influence on those composers – Mily Balakirev, César Cui, Modest Mussorgsky, Nikolai Rimsky-Korsakov and Alexander Borodin – who were known as the Five and introduced the concept of a true Russian music. He wrote two great operas, *A Life for the Tsar* in 1836, about a Russian patriotic hero who sacrifices his life for the tsar, and *Ruslan and Lyudmila* in 1842, based on a poem by Pushkin in which the daughter of the Prince of Kiev is abducted by a villainous dwarf. He was responsible for the introduction of Russian music into the opera house for the first time and the music for dancers and chorus within the opera anticipate Borodin's Polovtsian Dances in *Prince Igor*.

> **DID YOU KNOW?**
> Tchaikovsky called Glinka 'the acorn from which the oak of Russian music sprang'.

Michael William Balfe (1808–1870)

Michael Balfe was an Irishman, son of a Dublin dancing master and violinist, and he himself played the violin on stage at the age of eight. He went to London aged sixteen and became a violinist at the Drury Lane Theatre, and then to Italy, where he studied further and wrote his first stage work, a ballet, *Il Naufragio di La Perouse*, produced in Milan in 1825. He went to Paris where he met Rossini and studied singing under Bordogni, making his operatic debut as Figaro in *Il barbiere di Seviglia*. He became a popular singer in Italy and wrote his first comic opera, *I Rivali di se stessi*, in 1830 in Palermo. Two more followed and he returned to England, where he wrote *The Siege of Rochelle* for Drury Lane Theatre, followed by *The Maid of Artois*, a sensational success. His next three operas did less well and he went to Paris where he met the librettist Scribe, with whom he wrote two successes, *Le Puits d'Amour* and *Les Quatre Fils Aymon*. Back in

London at Drury Lane he produced his most successful opera, *The Bohemian Girl*, in 1842. This was followed in quick succession by *The Daughter of St Mark, The Enchantress, The Bondman, The Maid of Honour* and *The Sicilian Bride*. His travels in the 1850s were extensive, including Berlin, Vienna, Trieste and St Petersburg. On his return to England he was commissioned to write several new operas, including *The Rose of Castile, Satanella* and *The Puritan's Daughter*.

DID YOU KNOW?
Balfe went to Italy at the age of sixteen because an Italian nobleman, Count Mazzara, thought he showed such a strong resemblance to his recently deceased son that he wanted to show him to his family.

Franz von Suppé (1810–1895)

Von Suppé was born in Split in Dalmatia but he moved to Vienna and became the epitome of composers of Viennese operetta. He became the conductor at the Theater in der Josefstadt – at first without pay – and composed incidental music for plays and, eventually, his own operettas to be performed there and at the Theater an der Wien. His works include *Dichter und Bauer* (*Poet and Peasant*), *Das Pensionat, Flotte Burschen, Boccaccio, Donna Juanita, Leichte Kavallerie* (*Light Cavalry*), *Bellman* and *Die Frau Meisterin*. Von Suppé's work has subsequently appeared in some unlikely places, including cartoons! *Poet and Peasant* is used in a 1935 Popeye film and *Light Cavalry* in a 1942 Mickey Mouse cartoon called *Symphony Hour*.

William Vincent Wallace (1812–1865)

Born in Waterford, Ireland, Wallace learned to play several instruments as a boy and in 1828 became a violinist at the Theatre Royal in Dublin. He taught piano at the Ursuline Convent, where he fell in love with and married a pupil, Isabella Kelly. In 1835 the couple, with their infant son, Wallace's sister Elisabeth, a soprano, and his brother Wellington, a flautist, emigrated to Australia and opened the country's first music school in Sydney. His travels did not end here. Estranged from his wife, he went to New Zealand and various South Pacific islands and then to South America (rumoured to be fleeing from his debts in Australia). In 1841 he conducted Italian opera in Mexico, then went to the United States, where he helped to found the New York Philharmonic Society. In 1845 he was in London where his opera, *Maritana*, was produced at Drury Lane Theatre, revived three years later with his sister Elisabeth in the title role at Covent Garden. Further operas included *Matilda of Hungary*, *Lurline*, *The Amber Witch*, *Love's Triumph* and *The Desert Flower*.

Richard Wagner (1813–1883)

The greatest nineteenth-century German opera composer – arguably the greatest German composer ever – Wagner revolutionized the art form so that it could never be the same again. The creator of 'music drama', Wagner's early music obeyed the conventions of the day and it was not until 1843 and *Der Fliegende Hollander* (*The Flying Dutchman*) that he began to consolidate his unique vision and style, moving away from naturalistic drama to myth and symbolism. Two years later *Tannhäuser* appeared, and then *Lohengrin*, which was to confirm the direction he wanted to pursue. It was first performed in Weimar, conducted by Liszt, and Wagner followed it with *Tristan und Isolde*, a failure at the time but now regarded as a romantic masterpiece. In 1864 he had the inestimable good fortune to gain the patronage of King Ludwig of Bavaria, without whose backing it is unlikely Wagner would ever have seen his later work staged during his lifetime. *Der Meistersing von Nürnberg* (*The Mastersingers of Nuremberg*) was premiered in 1868 while Wagner's ultimate composition took over twenty years. The first part of the Ring appeared in 1869 but it was not until 1876 that the entire cycle was performed at Bayreuth, a theatre designed by the composer himself. Wagner wrote his own libretti, and designed the scenery and lighting – this was to be a complete artwork in which all the elements of staging, music and poetry were fused to produce an almost religious experience. His final opera, *Parsifal*, appeared in Bayreuth in 1882, just a year before Wagner's death.

DID YOU KNOW?
There have been a number of films about Wagner, the earliest a silent film in 1913. Later portrayals include Richard Burton as the composer in a TV mini-series, *Wagner*, Lyndon Brook in the 1960 film *Song without End* and an eccentric characterization in Ken Russell's *Lisztomania*, by Paul Nicholas.

Giuseppe Verdi (1813–1901)

Verdi is widely regarded as the greatest composer of Italian opera, his work epitomized by its drama, humanity and often brilliantly drawn characters. Born in the same year as Wagner, the two composers could not have been more different, both in terms of their music and the subjects to which they were drawn. Verdi opposes Wagner's symbolism and mythology with profoundly human dramas – indeed melodramas – and emotions. He was born in a village near Parma in Italy, the son of the local inn-keeper. He studied in Milan with Vincenzo Lavigna, a conductor at La Scala, but returned to Busseto near Parma where he became Director of the Philharmonic Society and wrote his first opera, *Oberto*. He also married and had two children but within a remarkably short period of time both his children and his wife died. Verdi decided to turn his back on opera, but was persuaded to write another for La Scala. This was *Nabucco*, his first major success, in 1843. A passionately told biblical story, it also had strong resonances for an Italian audience then under foreign rule. *I Lombardi*, *Ernani*, *Macbeth* and *Luisa Miller* followed but in the early 1850s politics were abandoned in favour of deeply human dramas and three masterpieces with a wealth of melody and strong storylines were the result: *Rigoletto*, *Il Trovatore* and *La Traviata*. The third period of Verdi's creativity was heralded in 1871 with *Aida*. Expected by many (perhaps also Verdi himself) to be his final masterpiece, he continued composing and, teaming up with librettist Arrigo Boiti, produced two extraordinary works of great depth and drama, based on Shakespeare plays: *Otello* and *Falstaff*, composed when Verdi was almost eighty.

DID YOU KNOW?
Giuseppe Verdi translates as 'Joe Greens', a joke used by the musical comedian Victor Borge and by Agatha Christie in *Evil Under the Sun*, in which it gives Poirot a clue to solving a murder mystery.

Charles Francois Gounod (1818–1893)

Gounod was born in Paris and was first given piano lessons by his mother, the daughter of a professor at the Conservatoire. His musical education continued in Rome and he composed a mass for the French church there. He returned to Paris, much influenced by polyphonic church music and Palestrina, as well as by a strong religious conviction and for some years he wrote only for the church. However, by 1851 he had written his first opera, *Sapho*. Gounod's graceful melodic music made him extremely popular in France during his lifetime and just about everywhere today. His *Faust*, composed in 1859, is his most widely performed opera and it focuses not on Goethe's play in its entirety but on the love story between Faust and Marguerite. Other popular works include *Le Médecin malgré Lui*, *Mireille* and *Romeo et Juliette*. Based on Shakespeare's play, the libretto follows the original closely and the music centred around the balcony scene – Romeo's initial aria and the duet for the two lovers – is quite lovely.

Jacques Offenbach (1819–1880)

Offenbach was actually Jakob Eberst, the son of a synagogue cantor in Cologne in the town of Offenbach-on-Main, but his witty, frivolous, satirical works made him be seen as the ultimate Parisian composer. Most of his astonishing number of works for the stage – around 100 – were operettas, the most famous including *Orphée aux Enfers* (*Orpheus in the Underworld* – a parody of Gluck's *Orphée*), *La Belle Hélène*, *La Vie Parisienne* (with its famous cancan), *La Grande Duchesse de Gérolstein* and *La Périchole*. His one true opera, *Les Contes d'Hoffman*, was unfinished at his death and scored only for piano. Orchestrated by Ernest Guiraud, it was

---

NEITZSCHE'S GENIUS

Friedrich Neitzsche said of Offenbach:

If by artistic genius we understand the most consummate freedom within the law, divine ease and facility in overcoming the greatest difficulties, then Offenbach has even more right to the title 'genius' than Wagner has. Wagner is heavy and clumsy, nothing is more foreign to him than the moments of wanton perfection which this clown Offenbach achieves as many as five times, six times, in nearly every one of his buffooneries.

---

premiered in Paris in 1881, and became an immediate favourite. He was the father of operetta and influenced everyone who worked in the genre, including Gilbert and Sullivan.

Edouard Lalo (1823–1892)

Success came very late to Edouard Lalo. Born in Lille, he trained as a string player and composed ballads and chamber music. It was his wife, the singer Mlle de Maligny, who persuaded him to write for the stage. His first attempt was *Fiesque* – a failure. His first success came in 1874 and 1875 in the shape of his Concerto in F and *Symphonie espagnol*, still popular in the concert hall today. His next opera was *Le Roi dYs* (*The King of Ys*), based on a Breton tale, but it was not performed until 1888 when it was recognized as his masterpiece.

Bedrich Smetana (1824–1884)

Although sometimes called 'the father of Czech music', when Smetana was alive there was neither a Czech republic nor a country called Czechoslovakia. He was born in what was then Bohemia and was to die at the age of sixty in its capital, Prague. The concept of nationalism, however, became a potent one in the middle of the nineteenth century and Smetana produced a series of operas with both suitably Bohemian subjects and music. This was after he had lived for some years in Sweden and on his return his music was at first far from popular and accused of being Wagnerian. However, his first opera, *The Brandenburgers in Bohemia*, premiered in 1866 was a populist triumph and was followed only months later by his most popular opera, *The Bartered Bride*. His other operas included *Dalibor*, *The Two Widows*, *The Kiss*, *The Secret*, *Libuse* and *The Devil's Wall*. Smetana wrote orchestral and piano scores too, but it is for his operas that he is best known.

DID YOU KNOW?

Smetana suffered for years from a condition which meant he heard a constant high note, then in 1874 he suddenly became completely deaf. He died in an asylum and was buried in a cemetery on the legendary site of Vysehrad, the castle of the mythical foundress of Prague, Libuse, who was the heroine of one of his operas.

Alexander Borodin (1833–1887)

Borodin was the illegitimate son of a prince and trained first in medicine, but he became interested in music on meeting Mussorgsky and this interest strengthened when he met Balakirev in 1862. He wrote his first opera in 1867, a parody of grand opera entitled *The Valiant Knights*. He worked on his masterpiece, *Prince Igor*, throughout the 1870s but it was left unfinished on his sudden death from a burst artery in the heart in 1887. It was finished, along with other incomplete works, by Rimsky-Korsakov and Glazunov. *Prince Igor* illustrates Borodin's interest in both Russian folk music and the Orient, most often seen in the Polovtsian Dances that became a popular hit for Diaghilev's *Ballets Russes*.

DID YOU KNOW?
Borodin did not neglect his medical training and became a professor of chemistry and the founder of a school of medicine for women.

Amilcare Ponchielli (1834–1886)

Ponchielli tends to be forgotten as he has been so overshadowed by the other two great Italian composers of the time, Verdi and Puccini – the latter actually being one of his own pupils. Clearly talented from an early age, he joined the Milan Conservatoire at the age of nine. His first opera, *I promessi sposi*, was composed when he was twenty-two and his second, *Roderico*, in 1863. In 1872 he rewrote *I promessi sposi* for the opening of the Teatro dal Verme in Milan and wrote a ballet and then an opera, *I Lituana*, for La Scala in 1874. In 1876 he composed his masterpiece, *La Giaconda*, the story of two women in love with the same man during the Inquisition. After this major success he wrote *Il figliul prodigo* and *Marion Delorme*, but it was *La Giaconda* that was to make his name and it is the only opera of his performed today.

Camille Saint-Saëns (1835–1921)

Born in Paris, Saint-Saëns was brought up by his mother and her aunt, both of whom recognized his musical gifts at an early age. He had already given his first professional piano recital before he entered the Paris Conservatoire in 1848. He was a prolific composer, his work ranging from orchestral music such as the symphonic poem *Danse Macabre*, piano and organ music and a number of operas. These include *Hélène*, the score of which was lost until 2007 and performed for the first time in 2008. His most famous opera is, though, *Samson et Dalila*, first performed in 1877.

Léo Delibes (1836–1891)

Delibes was born in Paris and entered the Conservatoire there at the age of twelve. One of his teachers was the composer of the ballet *Giselle*, Adolphe Adams, and Delibes himself is perhaps best known for his own ballet, *Coppélia*. He became the accompanist at the Theatre Lyrique and at the same time wrote a number of comic operettas. In 1863 he became accompanist at the Paris Opera and composed ballet music, including *Coppélia*, in 1870. He wrote two operas, *Hean de Nivelle* and *Le Roi l'a dit*, but his best-known work is *Lakmé* – one of the works that began opera's love affair with orientalism – which is famed for its beautiful duets. He did begin another opera, *Kassya*, but died before its completion. It was finished by Massenet, but is rarely performed.

DID YOU KNOW?

Most people – many of them never having listened to opera in their lives – are now familiar with Delibes, since British Airways used the barcarole from *Lakmé* as the theme tune to their advertising campaigns from the 1990s.

Georges Bizet (1838–1875)

Another short-lived composer – he died aged thirty-six – Bizet produced a series of operas of such melodic brilliance and dramatic intensity that they remain at the forefront of the repertoire in opera houses around the world today. Born in Paris, his early musical talent resulted in admittance to the Conservatoire while he was still only ten years old. He wrote his first symphony when he was just sixteen and won the Grand Prix de Rome, where he wrote his first opera, *Don Procopio*. His first major success was *Les Pêcheurs de Perles* (*The Pearl Fishers*) in 1863 with its hypnotically lyrical music. He followed this in 1867 with *La Jolie Fille de Perth* (*The Fair Maid of Perth*), based on the novel of the same name by Sir Walter Scott. But it was, of course, his final opera, *Carmen*, that was staged just a few weeks before his death that was to be his most enduring success. Technically, because of its spoken dialogue, *Carmen* is classified as an *opera comique*. It is in every other respect one of the great tragic dramas to have appeared on the operatic stage. At its Paris premiere, it was a failure, partly due to the licentiousness and brutality of its story and, more surprisingly, due to the difficulty of the music (the orchestra and the chorus both complained about it)! A few months after Bizet's death, it was acclaimed in Vienna, and went on to become arguably the most popular opera ever.

DID YOU KNOW?

After Bizet's death, his widow Geneviève married Emile Strause, a member of the Rothschild family. She became a famous society hostess and Proust used her as the inspiration behind the Duchesse de Guermentes in *A la recherche de temps perdu*.

Modest Petrovich Mussorgsky (1839–1881)

Mussorgsky drew on his native Russian history as themes for his two great operas, *Boris Godunov* and *Khovanshchina* (*The Khovansky Rising*). His musical and dramatic styles were equally unique for his times. Instead of the normal consecutive developing acts, he created a series of tableaux that presented an unfolding drama of vast historical proportions. The music for both operas, sometimes regarded as roughly hewn, was re-orchestrated by his friend Rimsky-Korsakov to make it more acceptable for tastes at the time. Over the years, though, Mussorgsky's own music was recognized as original and highly effective, and it is his version that is usually played today. Mussorgsky did make a start on several other operas, though he finished none of them.

AN UNCOUTH COMPOSER

Tchaikovsky wrote in a letter to his patroness Nadezhda von Meck:

Mussorgsky you very rightly call a hopeless case. In talent he is perhaps superior to all the [other members of The Five], but his nature is narrow-minded, devoid of any urge towards self-perfection, blindly believing in the ridiculous theories of his circle and in his own genius. In addition, he has a certain base side to his nature which likes coarseness, uncouthness, roughness ... He flaunts ... his illiteracy, takes pride in his ignorance, mucks along anyhow, blindly believing in the infallibility of his genius. Yet he has flashes of talent which are, moreover, not devoid of originality.

Peter Ilitsch Tchaikovsky (1840–1893)

Best known as a composer of orchestral and ballet music, Tchaikovsky was an important figure, too, in Russian opera in the nineteenth century. His happy early life was shattered when his mother died when he was fourteen and he found himself – despite obvious and early musical talent – first in a boarding school, then a clerk in the Ministry of Justice. At the age of twenty-two he took a major gamble and decided to become a musician. It paid off: he got a job at the newly opened St Petersburg Conservatoire teaching harmony and began composing. Symphonies and ballet music followed, none with quite the success at the time that they would receive later. Tchaikovsky was fortunate to find a patron, Madame Nadezhda von Meck, with whom he exchanged long, both professional and personal, letters and who supported him while he composed. His operatic masterpiece is, without doubt, *Eugene Onegin*, which contains music of great power and lyricism. His other most often-played opera is *The Queen of Spades*, a study in obsession, but he did write a number of other operas that, though more frequently staged in Russia, deserve to be heard more often elsewhere, too. These include *The Maid of Orleans* and *Mazeppa*.

A STINKING COMPOSER

Like so many composers, Tchaikovsky's early music was not understood or appreciated. The music critic Eduard Hanslick said of his first violin concerto:

> The Russian composer Tchaikovsky is surely no ordinary talent, but rather, an inflated one, obsessed with posturing as a man of genius, and lacking all discrimination and taste ... the same can be said for his new, long, and ambitious Violin Concerto. For a while it proceeds soberly, musically, and not mindlessly, but soon vulgarity gains the upper hand and dominates until the end of the first movement. The violin is no longer played: it is tugged about, torn, beaten black and blue ... The Adagio is well on the way to reconciling us and winning us over when, all too soon, it breaks off to make way for a finale that transports us to the brutal and wretched jollity of a Russian church festival. We see a host of gross and savage faces, hear crude curses, and smell the booze. In the course of a discussion of obscener illustrations, Friedrich Vischer once maintained that there were pictures whose stink one could see. Tchaikovsky's Violin Concerto confronts us for the first time with the hideous idea that there may be musical compositions whose stink one can hear.

Antonín Dvořák (1841–1904)

Along with Bedrich Smetana, best known as an opera composer for his *The Bartered Bride*, Dvořák was the mainstay of the nineteenth-century Czech movement that produced a new nationalist music. It drew deeply on the rhythms, tunes and instruments of the country's folk music, but was transposed by these composers into an orchestrated and far more polished style. Dvořák even used folk tales as the basis of his opera as in, for instance, *Rusalka*, his best-known work for the stage, which was an unusual choice of subject in Prague at the time. The folk tales he used were not, however, particularly Czech in origin, being a combination of French fairy stories and Hans Christian Andersen. Altogether, Dvorák composed thirteen operas, though most are seldom performed outside his native land. Generally, he is better known as a composer of orchestral music.

DID YOU KNOW?
Just as Mozart married Constanze, the sister of his first love Aloysia, Dvorák married Anna, the sister of his own first love, Josefina.

Jules Massenet (1842–1912)

Massenet, having been taught the piano by his musical mother, entered the Paris Conservatoire at the age of eleven. His first opera, *La grand'tante*, appeared at the Opéra-Comique in 1867 and more soon followed – *Le Roi de Lahore*, *Hérodiade*, *Esclarmonde*, *Thaïs*, *Cendrillon*, *Werther*, *Le Jongleur de Notre Dame*, *La Navarraise*, *Thérèse*, *Sapho*, *Don Quichotte*, *Roma* and, most successful and enduring of all, *Manon*. Massenet drew on many contemporary themes, both musical and literary – the exotic and the Bohemian rub shoulders with influences as disparate as Wagner and Meyerbeer. He is most remembered, though, for his sweet melodic lines and his magnificent heroines.

DID YOU KNOW?
Massenet was elected a member of the Académie des Beaux-Arts in 1878 when he was only thirty-six, then the youngest-ever member.

Arthur Sullivan (1842–1900)

A chorister at the Chapel Royal, Arthur Sullivan was a musical child prodigy, going on to study at the Royal Academy of Music and then in Leipzig, where he developed a passion for Schubert's music, which he singlehandedly introduced to England when he returned in 1861. He composed a ballet and church music but soon was drawn to operetta. In 1871 he met WS Gilbert and though their first collaboration, *Thespis*, was not a success, they worked together a few years later and produced *Trial by Jury*. This took the town by storm and in 1877 Richard D'Oyly Carte founded his company to produce the works of Gilbert and Sullivan: a unique combination of Gilbert's witty librettos – often satirically directed towards everything from the aesthetic movement to the law – and Sullivan's melodic and often equally witty musical scores. Their most famous collaborations include *The Pirates of Penzance*, *Patience*, *Iolanthe*, *Princess Ida*, *The Mikado*, *Ruddigore*, *The Yeomen of the Guard* and *The Gondoliers*.

A KNIGHTED COMPOSER

When Sullivan was knighted in 1883, it was felt in some quarters that he ought to abandon the comic operas for which he was so famed and get down to something more serious. The *Musical Review* opined:

> Some things that Mr Arthur Sullivan may do, Sir Arthur ought not to do. In other words, it will look rather more than odd to see announced in the papers that a new comic opera is in preparation, the book by Mr W. S. Gilbert and the music by Sir Arthur Sullivan. A musical knight can hardly write shop ballads either; he must not dare to soil his hands with anything less than an anthem or a madrigal; oratorio, in which he has so conspicuously shone, and symphony, must now be his line. Here is not only an opportunity, but a positive obligation for him to return to the sphere from which he has too long descended.

Nicolai Rimsky-Korsakov (1844–1908)

Rimsky had planned as a child to become a sailor and enrolled in the St Petersburg Naval College at the age of twelve. He had previously learned the piano but it was not until he went to the opera that he started composing – re-writing the Persian music from Donizetti's *Ruslan* for cello and piano. However, he had to go into the navy for three years (he was to remain involved with the navy throughout his life, eventually becoming Inspector of Naval Bands) and he arrived back home at twenty-one, became friends with Mussorgsky and wrote his first symphony. He became Professor of Composition and Instrumentation at the St Petersburg Conservatory at the age of twenty-seven and continued writing symphonies and such famous pieces as *Spanish Capriccio* and *Scheherazade*. It was much later in his life that he started to compose operas – *Christmas Eve*, *Sadko*, *Mozart and Salieri*, *The Tsar's Bride*, *Servilia*, *The Invisible City of Kitezh* and *The Golden Cockerel*. His music is marked by his love of orientalism and Russian folk song. Although less known than his orchestral music, Rimsky considered his operas to be his masterpieces, and they are gradually becoming better known in the west.

DID YOU KNOW?

Rimsky was an important teacher and counted among his pupils Glazunov, Prokofiev, Stravinsky and Respighi.

Engelbert Humperdinck (1854–1921)

Engelbert Humperdinck is best known for his opera *Hansel und Gretel*. It was written at the request of his sister, who had written a play for children based on the fairy tale by the brothers Grimm: she asked him to write some incidental music. Humperdinck became so involved he made it into a full-length opera and it was premiered in Weimar in 1893 and acclaimed a masterpiece by Richard Strauss. It became the first opera broadcast on the radio both in Europe (1923) and America (1931). He wrote a good deal of incidental music for the theatre but only one more opera, *Königskinder* (*The Royal Children*).

> **DID YOU KNOW?**
> The sixties pop singer (real name was Arnold George Dorsey) stole the composer's name when his manager suggested he needed a more eye-catching moniker. It paid off in 1967 with the number one-hit 'Release Me'.

Alfredo Catalani (1845–1893)

Catalani was extremely popular in his day but, because he composed in what was regarded as an old-fashioned manner, shunning the *verismo* style, he lost his place – many would say unfairly – in the repertoire. A typically lyrical Italian composer, his most famous operas are *La Wally* (1892) and *Loreley* (1890). His other operas, less successful given their weaker librettos, include *La Falce* (*The Sickle*), *Elda*, *Dejanice* and *Edmea*.

> **DID YOU KNOW?**
> The conductor Toscanini was a great admirer of Catalani's music and not only was he involved in its performance, but he called his daughter Wally after Catalini's heroine.

Leos Janacek (1854–1928)

Janacek was born in Moravia, now part of the Czech Republic, and became a chorister in Brno and choirmaster at the age of sixteen. At the monastery school he attended he was much influenced by a monk, Pavel Krizovsky, who was also a composer of decidedly nationalist tendencies. In his twenties, Janacek wrote orchestral and choir music, studied folk music and taught, but it was not for some time that he would write the music that would bring him renown. His first opera, *Jenúfa*, was first performed in Brno in 1904 when he was fifty and while it was a triumph there it was to take another twelve years before the National Theatre in Prague would produce it. Janacek continued composing, however. In 1914, *Mr Broucek's Excursions* was staged, a delightful, fantastical piece in which the hero visits the moon in a dream. Piano, orchestral music and string quartets appeared rapidly, as did another four operas. In 1919 he wrote *Katya Kabanova*, partly as a result of his unreciprocated infatuation for Kamila Stösslová, the wife of a friend. *The Makropoulos Affair* followed a few years later, then the charming *The Cunning Little Vixen* and *The House of the Dead*, based on Dostoevsky's story of life in a Siberian prison. All of Janacek's music is epitomized by its highly individual voice, combining Gregorian chant, folk music, vitality and lyricism.

Ruggiero Leoncavallo (1857–1919)

Ruggiero Leoncavallo's best-known – and indeed best – work, *Pagliacci*, is often teamed with *Cavalleria Rusticana*, both being short but highly effective examples of the *verismo* movement in Italian opera. Leoncavallo wrote his first opera, *Chatterton*, as a teenager and after *Pagliacci* went on to compose *I Medici* – planned as the first part of a trilogy, but which he gave up as a failure – and, just months before Puccini, a version of *La Bohème*, which was based on the same story and played at the Teatro la Fenice in Venice. Though quite well received at the premiere, it inevitably suffered by comparison with Puccini's version. He went on to write several more operas, the best of which is *Zazà*, as well as operettas, but it is *Pagliacci* for which he will always be known.

Giacomo Puccini (1858–1924)

It was Verdi who made Puccini a composer of operas. When he saw *Aida* in 1876, the young Puccini knew that this was what he wanted to do. Previously destined to be a church composer and organist – a family tradition – Puccini studied at the Conservatorio Reale in Milan and while still a pupil there entered a competition for a one-act opera. He wrote *Le Villi* – the legend of brides deserted by their lovers who turn into ghosts who dance their beloved to death, which was, of course, the same story as the great ballet *Giselle*. It was staged in 1884 at the Teatro dal Verme and was an instant success. His next work was the far less well-received *Edgar*, but he followed this with *Manon Lescaut* and his reputation was made. Puccini is Verdi's natural successor, a composer of the human drama and magnificent music, considered by many to be the last truly great Italian composer of opera. While these two elements are at the core of Puccini's operas, there were several other influences. The *verismo* school of Italian realism is evident in *Tosca* and *La Bohème* while in *Madama Butterfly* and *Turandot* the exoticism of the east informs both the music and the drama. If it was his third opera, *Manon Lescaut*, that catapulted him to international fame, its three successors – *La Bohème*, *Tosca* and *Madama Butterfly* – secured his position as a master of his art. Best known for passionate melodrama, Puccini could write comedy too, for instance in the one-act opera *Gianni Schicchi*. A series of operas followed that are less well known today but are sometimes performed: *La Fanciulla del West* (*The Girl of the Golden West*), *La Rondine* (*The Swallow*), *Il Tabarro* (*The Cloak*), *Suor Angelica* (*Sister Angelica*) and *Gianni Schicchi*. His final opera, *Turandot*, is regarded by many as his masterpiece, though others argue for *Madama Butterfly* and still others for *La Bohème*, and is nowadays known far beyond regular opera-going circles as the World Cup theme sung by Pavarotti. This is perhaps fitting. Puccini was always a profoundly popular composer and his soaring arias for tenors and especially sopranos are some of the best-loved and best-known moments of opera still.

Claude Debussy (1862–1918)

As one of the foremost composers in the development of orchestral impressionism, Debussy was extremely influential in a number of musical genres. He wrote only one opera, *Pelléas et Mélisande*, which groundbreaking both musically and dramatically, working on almost a subconscious, intuitive level rather than through a developing plot. It had many detractors at the time, though it went on to become a regularly performed opera around the world. He is better known as a composer of piano, orchestral and ballet music – his *Prélude à L'après-midi d'un faune* is cited by many musicologists as the first truly modern piece of music. The piece was based on the poem of the same name by Mallarmé and only turned into a ballet two decades later when the *Ballets Russes* under Diaghilev created a scandal with Nijinsky's clearly erotic interpretation of the piece.

Pietro Mascagni (1863–1945)

Though forbidden by his father to study music, Pietro Mascagni managed to do so with the help of a kind uncle who took him in, composing a symphony and kyrie that were performed when he was just sixteen. He studied at the Milan Conservatoire but did not like it and left to work as a conductor in a travelling opera company. He wrote *Cavalleria Rusticana* when he was just twenty-six and it was submitted for a competition, winning first prize and premiering in Rome with resulting huge success. It is a masterly achievement, a favourite in the repertoire where, as it is just one act, it usually plays as part of a double bill. The passion, musical inspiration and dramatic libretto of this early opera was, sadly, never revisited and Mascagni never repeated his early success. It did, however, begin a new trend within Italian opera for *verismo* or dramatic realism.

DID YOU KNOW?
Mascagni was aware he peaked early, once declaring, 'It was a pity I wrote *Cavalleria* first. I was crowned before I was a king.'

Richard Strauss (1864–1949)

Richard Strauss was not a relation of the Johann Strausses and the rest of that esteemed musical family of Vienna. He was born in Munich, the son of Franz Strauss, a renowned horn player, and at the age of six had already embarked on composing. He met the famous conductor Hans von Bülow in 1883, who played the young composer's Wind Serenade with the Meiningen Court Orchestra, and Strauss became the orchestra's assistant music director as a result. Strauss's tone poems and operatic scores were highly original and he is often regarded as the last great German romantic composer. His first opera, *Guntram*, was not a success in Munich and Strauss left for Berlin to pursue his conducting career, though he still did a great deal of composing. His next two operas, *Salome* and *Elektra*, were considered revolutionary both in terms of subject matter and music – far stronger and more ferocious than opera-goers at the time were expecting. His next opera was utterly different, the magical *Der Rosenkavalier*, which features a beguiling Viennese waltz, a comic plot and plenty of disguises. Strauss became Director of the State Opera in Vienna in 1919 and he was to write many more operas, the best known being *Arabella*. His final work was for the voice, the song cycle Four Last Songs, and he was working on a fifth when he died.

A FOOLISH COMPOSER

Saint-Saëns did not appreciate Strauss's work. He wrote:

The desire to push works of art beyond the realm of art means simply to drive them into the realm of folly. Richard Strauss is in the process of showing us that road.

Ferruccio Busoni (1866–1924)

Busoni had an Italian father, a clarinetist, and an Austrian mother, a pianist, both of whom taught him music, and by his mid-teens he was a formidable pianist himself. He played concerts and also composed and taught, travelling to perform from the United States to Moscow. The First World War, however, put an end to his travels and, based in Berlin, he completed his first opera, *Die Brautwahl*, in 1911. This was followed in 1917 by *Arlecchino* and *Turandot* – drawn from the same original fairytale by Carlo Gozzi as Puccini's opera of the same name. His masterpiece, however, is generally thought to be *Doktor Faust*, which, left unfinished at his death, was completed by his student Philipp Jarnach and later expanded by Antony Beaumont.

Francesco Cilèa (1866–1950)

Cilèa's first opera, *Gina*, was produced in 1889 while he was still a student at the Naples Conservatoire and brought him the commission for his second, *La Tilda*. In 1897 *L'Arlesiana* premiered in Milan and brought Enrico Caruso to public attention for the first time. In 1902 Cilèa wrote his masterpiece, *Adriana Lecouvreur*, based on a true – though melodramatized – story of a famous French actress, the mistress of a count at the court of Louis XV.

Umberto Giordano (1867–1948)

Giardano studied at the Naples Conservatoire and wrote his first opera, *Marina*, at the age of twenty-two. He entered it for the competition that was won by Mascagni's *Cavalleria Rusticana*. His next opera, *Mala Vita*, was premiered in Rome in 1892 to great acclaim and was very much of the same *verismo* school as Leoncavallo and Mascagni himself. In 1894 he wrote *Regina Diaz*, which was not a success, but he made his name two years later with *Andrea Chénier*. The story of a poet during the French Revolution, it was premiered at La Scala and became an instant success and was staged internationally as far afield as Moscow and New York in the same year. This was Giordano's most enduring work and his later operas – *Fedora*, *Madame Sans-Gêne* and *La Cena delle Beffe* – are rarely heard, though *Andrea Chénier* remains firmly in the repertoire. His students included Otto Klemperer and Carl Orff.

DID YOU KNOW?
Giordano was so beloved in Italy that his funeral cortege stopped outside La Scala and the coffin was placed in the doorway while the orchestra played 'Amor di vieta' from *Fedora*.

Hans Pfitzner (1869–1949)

Pfitzner was born in Moscow but spent most of his life in Germany and was a self-declared anti-modernist, calling himself rather 'the last romantic'. He wrote many delicate lieder and his first opera, *Der Arme Heinrich*, was first performed in 1899 in Mainz. His second opera was *Die Rose von Liebsgarten* (subtitled 'a romantic opera') and in 1906 he wrote the incidental music for the play *Das Christelflein* that he later turned into a comic opera. His operatic masterpiece is generally held to be *Palestrina*, written in 1917. He wrote one further opera, *Das Herz: A Drama for Music*. Though his work fell from favour from the 1930s, Pfitzner's operas and his violin concerto have begun to reappear in the repertoire and Werner Andreas Albert has conducted all of his orchestral works for recordings.

Franz Lehár (1870–1948)

Lehár's father was a bandmaster in the Austrian Army so the young Franz was constantly on the move until he went to the Music Academy in Prague at the age of twelve. He was best known at the Academy as a violinist but, when he showed his early compositions to Dvořák and Brahms, he was given plenty of encouragement. At twenty he became an army bandmaster like his father but carried on composing, including an opera, *Kukuschka*, which was performed in Leipzig, Budapest and Vienna. Lehár moved to Vienna himself where he found himself drawn more to operetta than opera and after a few earlier efforts in 1905 wrote the work that was to make his name, *Die Lustige Witwe* (*The Merry Widow*). His next works were greeted with great acclaim but over the years Lehár's compositions seemed to lose their lustre until he met Richard Tauber, the great tenor of the day, and he began to compose with Tauber in mind. He created a series of operettas including *Paganini*, *The Tsarevich*, *Friederike* and *Das Land des Lächelns* (*The Land of Smiles*). Their final collaboration was on *Giuditta*, a glittering affair in 1934, but soon to be overshadowed by the Second World War. Tauber left for England and Lehár and his Jewish wife, Sophie, went to their villa in Bad Ischl, though it was only Lehár's influence with the local Nazi chief that saved her.

94

DID YOU KNOW?
The Merry Widow has been made into a film three times – though sometimes rather a long way from the original. The most recent starred Lana Turner and Fernando Lamas in 1952. The most unlikely, by Erich von Stroheim, starred John Gilbert and Mae Murray – in a silent version.

Ralph Vaughan Williams (1872–1958)

Vaughan Williams is mostly renowned as an orchestral composer but he did write choral works, songs and several operas. He studied music at the Royal College of Music in London and with Max Bruch and Ravel and was a lifelong student of English folk music and English Tudor music. His *Sea Symphony* of 1910 was a choral–orchestral work based on Walt Whitman's poems, as were *Benedicite*, *Magnificat*, *Five Tudor Portraits* and *Dona nobis pacem*. The first of his operas – all, like so much of his music, with a truly English idiom – was *The Shepherds of the Delectable Mountains* in 1922, followed by *Hugh the Drover*, *Sir John in Love*, *The Poisoned Kiss*, *Riders to the Sea* and *The Pilgrim's Progress*.

DID YOU KNOW?
Vaughan Williams was on a tour in 1904 collecting English folk tunes when he visited Horsham in West Sussex. There he met Henry Burstow, a cobbler who knew some 420 songs by heart, Mr Penfolk, the landlord of the Plough Inn at Rusper, and the Verralls of the nearby village of Monk's Gate. He recorded in note form and on the phonograph sixteen songs and it was one of these that he used for the hymn 'He Who Would Valiant Be'.

Arnold Schoenberg (1874–1951)

Schoenberg is not principally known as an opera composer but he did write four and his influence on other contemporary opera composers has been great. He was born in Vienna to Jewish parents but was later to convert to Christianity. To support his family after the death of his father, he had to work for a while in a bank, but by the end of the century he was earning his living from his music as a composer, teacher and conductor, with pupils who included Alban Berg and Anton von Webern. He had already stretched the boundaries of tonality but in 1908 he abandoned it altogether in the song *Du lehnest wider eine Silberweide*. The initial response of public and critics was not promising, but Schoenberg continued on his new course and moved to Berlin where his work found more favour, Busoni conducting *Pierrot Lunaire*. In 1913, he had his first popular success with the *Gurrelieder*. He wrote four operas in all: *Erwartung* (*Expectation*) in 1909; *Die glückliche Hand* (*The Lucky Hand*), finished in 1928; *Von Heute auf Morgen* (*From Today to Tomorrow*) in 1929; and over the next three years *Moses und Aron*. The rise of the Nazis forced Schoenberg to flee Berlin and he moved to France, returning to the Jewish faith, in 1933 and then to New York and later California, where he taught at the University of California, Los Angeles (UCLA).

DID YOU KNOW?

Schoenberg suffered from triskaidekaphobia – the fear of the number thirteen. For this reason he changed the original spelling of his opera *Moses und Aaron* because it had thirteen letters. He died shortly before midnight on Friday 13 July 1951.

Maurice Ravel (1875–1937)

Ravel's exquisite orchestral music is quintessentially French. He studied at the Paris Conservatoire and stayed on to try to win the Prix de Rome, but conservative elements thought his work too radical and, despite being the favourite, he lost out to Victor Gallois. Ravel's early works include *Jeux d'eau* for piano, a string quartet and songs and, in 1902, *Pavane pour une infante défunte*, widely acknowledged as a masterpiece. He was much influenced by Spanish music and wrote his first 'Spanish piece', *Rhapsodie espagnole*, in 1907. Ultimately, this led to his Spanish opera, *L'Heure espagnole* (*The Spanish Hour*), in the same year. Piano, orchestral music and ballets followed, most notably *Daphnis et Chloé*, written for Diaghilev's *Ballets Russes*, with choreography by Michel Fokine and designs by Leon Bakst. In 1925 he finished his second opera, with a libretto by Colette, *L'Enfant et les Sortiléges*. His most successful and controversial work, *Boléro*, was written in 1928.

DID YOU KNOW?

Ravel and Debussy knew each other well but did not welcome the continuous comparisons made between them. Ravel wrote that Debussy's:

genius was obviously one of great individuality, creating its own laws, constantly in evolution, expressing itself freely, yet always faithful to French tradition. For Debussy, the musician and the man, I have had profound admiration, but by nature I am different from Debussy.

Manuel de Falla (1876–1946)

De Falla was born in Cadiz in Spain and moved to Madrid with his family aged twenty, where he passed the Conservatory exams and wrote *zarzuela*, or Spanish light opera, such as *Los amores de la Inés*. He wrote his first true opera in 1905, *La vida breve* (*Life is Short*), and though it won first prize in a competition it failed to get a performance and de Falla set off to Paris. Here, he met Debussy, Ravel and Stravinsky and had *La vida breve* performed in Nice and Paris. He returned to Madrid at the outbreak of the First World War and wrote a number of compositions that are still in the repertoire today, including two ballets, *El amor brujo* (*Love is a Witch*) and *El Sombrero de tres picos* (*The Three-cornered Hat*). The last was written for Diaghilev's *Ballets Russes* and it was premiered in London in 1919 with choreography by Massine and designs by Picasso. He became friends with the great Spanish poet Lorca, and with him wrote a puppet opera, *Master Peter's Puppet Show*. He settled in Argentina in 1939.

Ottorino Respighi (1879–1936)

Although perhaps best known as a composer of orchestral music – his trio of symphonic poems known as his *Roman Trilogy*: *The Fountains of Rome*, *The Pines of Rome* and *Festivals of Rome* (*Fontane di Roma*, *Pini di Roma* and *Feste Romane*) are widely played still – Respighi made his name writing operas and during the course of his life wrote nine of them. The first two, *Re Enzo* and *Semirama*, made his reputation and were instrumental in making him professor of composition at the Conservatorio Santa Cecilia in Rome. He was born in Bologna and, except for a brief few months in Russia as principal violinist of the Russian Imperial Theatre in St Petersburg, he lived in Italy all of his life, dying in Rome at the age of fifty-six. His other operas are *Marie Victoire*, *La bella dormente nel bosco*, *Belfagor*, *La campana sommersa*, *Maria Egiziaca*, *La fiamma* and *Lucrezia*.

Béla Bartók (1881–1945)

Bartók was born in a village that was then in Hungary but is now in Romania. He studied at the Budapest Academy and had shown immense musical promise from an early age, composing from the age of nine. He was much influenced by Liszt, Wagner and Strauss – he heard the latter's *Thus Spake Zarathustra* when he was twenty-one and his composition thereafter took a strongly Straussian turn for a while. He was even more influenced by Hungarian folk music, however, and spent many years collecting and cataloguing it – often with his lifelong friend and fellow composer Zoltán Kodály – and it was inevitably to influence his composition. The folk music did not rely on conventional scales and Bartók was to introduce previously unheard-of harmonies. He wrote several ballets, piano, chamber and orchestral music but only one opera. The one-act *Duke Bluebeard's Castle* was written while the composer was teaching at the Budapest Academy.

DID YOU KNOW?
Until Bartók's study of old Magyar, or Hungarian, folk melodies, they had generally been assumed to be part of a gypsy tradition. Bartók discovered they were, in fact, based on pentatonic scales similar to those of oriental folk music.

Zoltán Kodály (1882–1967)

Kodály was born in central Hungary and his compositions are strongly influenced by the folk songs of his country. He researched his native music and recorded it on cylinders, often going on these musical journeys with his friend Bartók. He wrote mostly chamber and orchestral music and he became a national musical icon throughout Hungary, even inventing a system for teaching music that was adopted throughout the country. His operas are *Háry János* and *The Transilvanian Spinning Room*.

Igor Federovich Stravinsky (1882–1971)

Stravinsky was born just outside St Petersburg and, though his father was an opera singer, he refused to see his son follow a musical career and so the young man trained as a lawyer. A meeting with Rimsky-Korsakov when Stravinsky was twenty changed all that and for the next six years he became Rimsky's student. In 1909 Stravinsky met the impresario of the *Ballets Russes*, Serge Diaghilev, and produced for him numerous ballet scores, as well as concert pieces and operas, the most famous of which are *The Firebird*, *Petrushka*, *Les Noces*, *The Nightingale* and *The Rite of Spring*. The last was to provoke a riot in the audience on the opening night, Stravinsky's music proving far more than they could cope with, its vigour, rhythm and harmony sounding as modern today as they did a century ago. *The Nightingale* was his earliest opera, but Stravinsky had a tendency to cross over genres. *The Soldier's Story* of 1917 combined music, dance and the spoken word. In 1927 he wrote *Oedipus Rex*, a secular oratorio, and in 1933 *Persephone*, an opera-ballet. His first full-scale opera was *The Rake's Progress*, first performed in 1951 in Venice. The works that followed were somewhat influenced by Webern and Schoenberg and most critics believe it is his earlier ones that best show his originality.

A NIGHTMARISH COMPOSER

Stravinsky was a stranger to critical acclaim for much of his life. In 1923, the *Musical Times* wrote:

> All the signs indicate a strong reaction against the nightmare of noise and eccentricity that was one of the legacies of the war ... What has become of the works that made up the program of the Stravinsky concert which created such a stir a few years ago? Practically the whole lot are already on the shelf, and they will remain there until a few jaded neurotics once more feel a desire to eat ashes and fill their belly with the east wind.

Sergei Sergeyevich Prokofiev (1891–1953)

Prokofiev first rose to prominence as a brilliant pianist and composer of piano music. A pupil of Rimsky-Korsakov at the St Petersburg Conservatory, he won the Rubinstein prize for his First Piano Concerto. However, during his lifetime he was to write piano and violin concertos, symphonies, ballets, film scores, the much-loved *Peter and the Wolf* and eleven operas, the first at the age of nine. His work is characterized by percussive rhythms, layers of harmony and melody, primitive emotions, energy and a striking sense of playfulness and wit. He wrote the music for two great classical ballets, *Romeo and Juliet* and *Cinderella*, as well as *The*

Prodigal Son and other less-performed work for the *Ballets Russes*, run by Diaghilev. His most often-performed opera today is *The Love of Three Oranges*, commissioned by the Chicago Opera, though it was not well received at the time. Others include *The Flaming Angel*, *War and Peace* and *The Story of a Real Man*. Prokofiev spent many years away from his native Russia, mostly in America, but returned there in 1934. Like so many Russian composers, his work was criticized by Stalin, and his last years were blighted by the attacks of the authorities for his 'modernism'. He was, though, restored to favour at the end, posthumously winning the Lenin Prize in 1957 for his Seventh Symphony and dying on the same day as Stalin in 1953.

DID YOU KNOW?

The Love of Three Oranges received mixed reviews on its first staging. One critic wrote, 'The work is intended, one learns, to poke fun. As far as I am able to discern it pokes fun chiefly at those who paid money for it.' However, it grew in popularity and was performed around the world. At the English National Opera production in the 1980s, the audience was given scratch 'n' sniff cards with smells to match on-stage events, such as gunshots, Truffaldino's 'wind' and, of course, oranges.

Alban Berg (1885–1935)

Berg was born in Vienna and died there at the age of fifty. He was generally regarded as the most popular of the 'second Viennese school' of composers, comprising Berg, Schoenberg and Webern. He was, in fact, a pupil of Schoenberg and while he embraced his teacher's atonality he did not follow his guidelines exclusively and his music is more lyrical and dramatic. He wrote song cycles and orchestral works and just two operas. The first, *Wozzeck*, was based on Büchner's play of the same name and was first performed in Berlin in 1925 and went on to tour twenty-nine cities, gradually gaining a foothold in the repertoire in spite of what many saw as the difficulty and modernism of the music. His second opera, *Lulu*, was unfinished when he died suddenly of blood poisoning following an insect bite. *Lulu* was based on two plays by Frank Wedekind, *The Earth Spirit* and *Pandora's Box*, and the first composer who was to finish the third act was to have been Schoenberg, but he later withdrew, possibly due to the handling of a Jewish character. Webern was also unable to complete the score and so the opera was performed for years in its unfinished state. However, in 1976, Berg's widow Helene – who had objected to some of the possible composers in the past – died and the opera was completed by Friedrich Cerha. It was finally premiered in its completed form in 1979 with Pierre Boulez conducting.

Heitor Villa-Lobos (1887–1959)

Villa-Lobos, without doubt the most significant Brazilian composer of the twentieth century, was born in Rio de Janeiro. His music is a vibrant mingling of the European classical tradition and Brazilian folk music. He had little conventional early training and was fascinated by the music around him. He absorbed early the different musical cultures – Portuguese, African, American Indian, and dances such as tangos and polkas – that were later to appear in his own compositions. He began composing seriously in his twenties with chamber and symphonic music. He was not, though, appreciated at home and so decided to go to Paris, where he gave concerts of his music and wrote *Douze Etudes* for Segovia, the great guitarist. He went on to write prolifically, his works including symphonies, concertos (for piano, guitar, harp and cello), chamber, choral and piano music, ballets, music for films and four works that are categorized both as operas and musicals: *Izaht*, *Magdalena*, *Yerma* and *Daughter of the Clouds*.

Darius Milhaud (1892–1974)

Milhaud studied at the Paris Conservatoire and was a member of Les Six. He was much influenced by jazz that he heard on a trip to the US in 1922. He emigrated to the US from his native France in 1940 and supported his composing by teaching at Mills College in Oakland, California. There he taught and influenced a wide range of musicians and composers, including Philip Glass and Steve Reich, Dave Brubeck and Burt Bacharach. He wrote chamber, orchestral, vocal and ballet music, film scores and opera. The operas include *Les euménides*, *Les Malheurs d'Orphée*, *Le Pauvre Matelot* (with a libretto by Jean Cocteau), *Christophe Colomb*, *Maximilien*, *Bolivar*, *Fiesta* and *Saint-Louis, roi de France*.

Carl Orff (1895–1982)

Best known for his oratorio *Carmina Burana*, Orff was also an opera composer, though he did not regard them as operas on a traditional model. With its primitive rhythms combined with the poems Orff discovered in the Benedictine monastery of Benedikbeuem, *Carmina Burana* proved irresistible to the public and Orff declared that he disowned his earlier work and this was the real start of his composing career. Folk, jazz and *Carmina Burana* idioms can all be heard in his later operas. These include *Der Mond* (*The Moon*) and *Die Kluge* (*The Wise Woman*), which he describes as 'fairytale operas', *Antigone* (a 'musical setting' of the tragedy) and *De Temporum Fine Comoedia* (*A Play at the end of Time*), described by Orff as a sung mystery play.

Paul Hindemith (1895–1963)

Hindemith was an important twentieth-century composer and he invented a unique musical system that is tonal but not diatonic, using a twelve-tone scale and ranking all musical intervals and chords from the most consonant to the most dissonant. His 1937 book *The Craft of Musical Composition* explained his system. His works includes chamber and symphonic music, song cycles and opera, and he was much in demand as a performer, a violinist, of his own and others' music. His first full-length opera was *Cardillac*, followed by *Mathis der Maler*, but this was not performed under the Nazi regime as Hindemith was accused of insulting Hitler and associating with Jewish musicians. In 1935 he left Germany and did not return until after the war. He wrote two operas after the war, *Die Harmonie der Welt* in 1957 and the one-act *The Long Christmas Dinner* in 1963, with a libretto by Thornton Wilder.

Virgil Thomson (1896–1989)

Virgil Thomson was born in Kansas City and, after the publication of his book *The State of Music*, became a music critic for the *New York Herald Tribune* from 1937 to 1951. He was also working from the thirties, however, as a composer for the stage and film. He wrote two operas with librettos by Gertrude Stein: *Four Saints in Three Acts* in 1928, famous at the time for its all-black cast, and, in 1947, *The Mother of us All*. He won the Pulitzer Prize for music in 1949 with his film score for *Louisiana Story*.

George Gershwin (1898–1937)

Gershwin's parents were Russian Jewish immigrants to New York and George became fascinated from an early age in the music of Harlem and ragtime, which he learned to play by ear. He did, though, go on to have classical lessons, but his formal education finished at age fifteen when he started working in Tin Pan Alley as a pianist and writing his own songs in his spare time. By 1919 his first musical had appeared – *La La Lucille* – and he soon had a reputation for writing such popular songs as 'I'll Build a Stairway to Paradise'. It was his *Rhapsody in Blue* of 1924, however, that was to bridge the gap between popular and classical, after which he wrote his Piano Concerto in F. In 1930 he went with his brother Ira, the lyric writer, to Hollywood and their partnership became legendary. His only true opera – and even this is disputed occasionally by purists because of its jazz idiom – is *Porgy and Bess*, produced in 1935, and still enormously popular today.

DID YOU KNOW?

Gershwin received his only Oscar nomination for Best Original Song in 1937 for 'They Can't Take That Away From Me' from the film *Shall We Dance*, but he died two months after the film's release.

Ernst Krenek (1900–1991)

Krenek studied composition with Franz Schreker at Vienna's Academy of Music and only began to explore atonality in his twenties. He was influenced, too, by Bartók and Mahler, to whose daughter, Anna, he was briefly married. He wrote orchestral, chamber, ballet and piano music, but

HOMAGE TO SCHUBERT

Krenek completed unfinished works by several other composers. Working from fragments for the third and fourth movements, he completed Schubert's *Reliquie* piano sonata and wrote on the sleeve notes of the 1947 recording:

Completing the unfinished work of a great master is a very delicate task. In my opinion it can honestly be undertaken only if the original fragment contains all of the main ideas of the unfinished work. In such a case a respectful craftsman may attempt, after an absorbing study of the master's style, to elaborate on those ideas in a way which to the best of his knowledge might have been the way of the master himself. The work in question will probably have analogies among other, completed works of the master, and careful investigation of his methods in similar situations will indicate possible solutions of the problems posed by the unfinished work. Even then the artist who goes about the ticklish task will feel slightly uneasy, knowing from his own experience as a composer that the creative mind does not always follow its own precedents. He is more conscious of the fact that unpredictability is one of the most jealously guarded prerogatives of genius ... However, scruples of this kind may be set aside once we are certain that the author of the fragment has put forth the essential thematic material that was expected to go into the work. If this is not the case, I feel that no one, not even the greatest genius, should dare to complete the fragments left by another genius.

is best known for his operas. His first was *Die Zwingburg* in 1922, followed by *Orpheus und Eurydike, Jonny spielt auf* (banned in Germany under the Nazis), *Der Diktator, Karl V*, and after his emigration to the United States in 1945 *What Price Confidence?, Dark Waters, The Bell Tower* and *Der Zauberspiegel*, an opera for television.

Aaron Copland (1900–1990)

Copland's parents were Russian Jews who emigrated to America but Aaron Copland embraced a range of American idioms, which makes his music instantly recognizable. Copland's music includes jazz and Latin American rhythms mingled with lyricism and soaring melodies and critics say his slowly changing harmonies evoke the great American landscapes. He is mostly known as an orchestral composer, but he wrote the music for many ballets, including *Appalachian Spring, El Salón México, Billy the Kid* and *Rodeo*. He also wrote two operas, *The Tender Land* and, for children, *The Second Hurricane*.

Kurt Weill (1900–1950)

Weill was born in Dessau in Germany and was a student of Albert Bing, Humperdinck and Busoni. He was a conductor for the opera house in Dessau and, though he wrote instrumental works, regarded himself principally as an opera composer, or at least a theatre composer, as his work took a very different path from that of conventional opera. He is best known for his collaboration with Bertolt Brecht, who had a similarly iconoclastic view that in stage works 'music should not co-operate in the action, but only interrupt it in suitable spots'. Their two greatest works were *The Threepenny Opera* and *The Rise and Fall of the City of Mahagonny*, a satire on a wicked mythical city that bore a curious resemblance to Berlin. These were huge popular successes when they appeared. However, the rise of Hitler made life difficult for the Jewish Weill and Lotte Lenya, Brecht's wife, and the three fled to Paris and then America. Here, Weill wrote an anti-war satire *Johnny Johnson*, and then succumbed to the bright lights of Broadway, writing a musical, *Knickerbocker Glory*, followed by *Lady in the Dark*, both hits. Other musicals – often with strong social messages –

included *Lost in the Stars,* based on the Alan Paton novel *Cry, the Beloved Country,* about racial tension in South Africa. He died while working on a musical adaptation of *Huckleberry Finn.*

William Walton (1902–1983)

William Turner Walton was born in Oldham, Lancashire and his musical career began when he became a chorister at Christ Church, Oxford. There, encouraged by the Dean, Thomas Banks Strong, and Professor Hugh Allen, he passed his Bachelor of Music exams very early and left at the tender age of sixteen. Thereafter, he was more or less self-taught. At university he met Sacheverell Sitwell and, through him, Osbert and Edith. The three Sitwells were at the forefront of artistic London at the time and took Walton under their wing. He wrote music, for instance, for Edith's poems – *Façade,* which later became a ballet. The large-scale choral work *Belshazzar's Feast* was very dramatic and brought Walton a good deal of public and critical attention. His opera *Troilus and Cressida* appeared in 1954 at the Royal Opera House, Covent Garden, conducted by Sir Malcolm Sargent. A one-act 'extravaganza', *The Bear,* based on a play by Anton Chekhov, was premiered at Aldeburgh in 1967.

Michael Tippett (1905–1998)

Tippett was born in London and in 1922 became a student at the Royal College of Music where he studied composition with Charles Wood and conducting with Adrian Boult and Malcolm Sargent. He was a late starter as a composer and frequently dissatisfied with his early work. An early ballad opera, *Robin Hood,* remains unpublished. At the age of thirty he started to produce compositions he seemed to find more acceptable, including his first string quartet, his Concerto for Double String Orchestra and the oratorio *A Child of our Time* in 1940. He became the head of the music department at London's Morley College (following in the footsteps of Holst) and wrote his first opera, *The Midsummer Marriage,* in its entirety – including the libretto – and it was produced at the Royal Opera House, Covent Garden, in 1955. Further operas, interspersed with orchestral compositions, include *King Priam, The Knot Garden, The Ice Break* and *New Year.*

Dmitri Dmitriyevich Shostakovich (1906–1975)

Shostakovich was born in St Petersburg and though his family were not professional musicians they were certainly musical, his mother having studied at the Conservatoire. She became his first piano teacher. His progress was rapid and, aged ten, he played for Glazunov, the Director of the St Petersburg Conservatoire, and was given a place studying piano and composition. He graduated at seventeen and began life as a professional composer with a great degree of success, his first symphony being heard even in the US. As a result, he became the first and much-valued 'Soviet composer' in the USSR. Unfortunately, his luck with the authorities was not to last. He was naturally interested in the work of other contemporary composers, both western and exiled Russians such as Prokofiev and Stravinsky, and this 'modernism' was strictly censured by Stalin, who wanted music to be popular and accessible to all. His first opera, *The Nose*, opened in 1929 but it was his second, *Lady Macbeth of Mtsensk*, that was attacked viciously by the Soviet authorities. For the rest of his life Shostakovich was caught in a dilemma and, while his later works of necessity towed the Party line, he was undoubtedly creatively limited by his masters. He nevertheless went on to write fifteen symphonies and nine string quartets, became an 'artistic war hero' and a teacher at the Moscow Conservatoire.

DID YOU KNOW?

Shostakovich was denounced twice by the Russian regime. First, in 1939, *Pravda* denounced *Lady Macbeth of Mtsensk* as 'coarse, primitive and vulgar'. In 1948 he was denounced for formalism along with many other composers in the Zhdanov decree and most of his works were banned, while he was forced to make a public admission of repentance.

Samuel Barber (1910–1981)

Born in Westchester, Pennsylvania, Samuel Barber studied at the Curtis Institute in Philadelphia and became a widely played composer of orchestral, piano and choral music as well as opera. His *Adagio for Strings* is probably his best-known work and he was twice awarded the Pulitzer Prize for music, once for his *Concerto for Piano and Orchestra* and once for his opera *Vanessa*. *Vanessa* was staged first at the Metropolitan Opera in New York in 1958 and at the Salzburg Festival the same year. The libretto was written by his partner, Gian Carlo Menotti. Barber wrote the opening opera – also with a libretto by Menotti – for the Lincoln Centre in New York in 1966: *Antony and Cleopatra*, in a production by Franco Zeffirelli.

THE 'MAD' COMPOSER

As a young boy Barber became aware of his vocation to be a composer but he was concerned that this was not what his family wanted. He wrote to his mother:

Dear Mother: I have written to tell you my worrying secret. Now don't cry when you read it because it is neither yours nor my fault. I suppose I will have to tell it now, without any nonsense. To begin with I was not meant to be an athlete. I was meant to be a composer, and will be I'm sure. I'll ask you one more thing. – Don't ask me to try to forget this unpleasant thing and go play football. – Please – Sometimes I've been worrying about this so much that it makes me mad (not very).

Gian-Carlo Menotti (1911–2007)

Though he was born in Italy and studied at the Verdi Conservatoire in Milan, Menotti moved to America at a young age and continued his studies there at the Curtis Institute in Philadelphia, receiving a Guggenheim Fellowship in 1947. He is known primarily as an opera composer and was unusual in that he wrote his own librettos. His operas have often played on Broadway and many are very popular, straddling both Italian and American trends. His first one-act opera was *Amelia Goes to the Ball* in 1937, followed by *The Island God*, *The Medium* and *The Telephone*. He won the Pulitzer Prize for two of his operas, *The Consul* and *The Saint of Bleeker Street*. He created the first television opera, *Amahl and the Night Visitors*, which has retained its popularity to this day, for Christmas 1951. In 1958 he founded the Spoleto Festival in Umbria, Italy, and in 1977 Spoleto Festival USA in South Carolina.

DID YOU KNOW?
In 1974, Menotti bought Yester House in East Lothian, Scotland, the ancestral home of the Marquess of Tweeddale, and called himself 'Mr McNotti' while in residence!

Benjamin Britten (1913–1976)

Britten began composing when he was just five years old and by the time he was ten had written six string quartets and ten piano sonatas. He was taught piano by Harold Samuel and composition by Frank Bridge before winning a scholarship to the Royal College of Music in London, where he studied with Arthur Benjamin for piano and John Ireland for composition. As a professional composer, he started by writing numerous songs as well as incidental music for documentary films, such as *Night Mail* with WH Auden, and stage. In 1939 he left England along with his friends Auden, Christopher Isherwood, the writer, and Peter Pears, the tenor. Pears and Britten went to Canada and then the US, where Britten collaborated with Auden again, this time on an operetta *Paul Bunyan*. His first opera was *Peter Grimes*, written on his return to his old house in Snape, Suffolk. Peter Pears played the title role when it appeared at Sadler's Wells in 1945 and became an overnight success. In rapid succession, Britten wrote the chamber opera *The Rape of Lucretia* and the comic opera *Albert Herring*. These two operas went on tour to European festivals and inspired Britten and Pears to start their own annual music festival at Aldeburgh. In 1948 he composed a new version of *The Beggar's Opera* and a year later *Let's Make an Opera*, for children. *Billy Budd* was commissioned by the Arts Council for the Festival of Britain in 1951 and *Gloriana* for the coronation of Queen Elizabeth II two years later, both at Covent Garden. *The Turn of the Screw* (1954), *A Midsummer Night's Dream* (1960) and *Owen Wingrave* (1970) followed. A later important influence on Britten was the music of the east, which he came across while touring in Bali, Japan and India in 1955. This is clear in his ballet *The Prince of the Pagodas* and in such works as *Curlew River*, based on a Japanese Noh play. His final opera was *Death in Venice*, based, of course, on the novel by Thomas Mann. He was created Baron Britten of Aldeburgh in 1976 and died a few months later of heart failure.

Leonard Bernstein (1918–1990)

A man of many talents, Bernstein excelled as composer, pianist and conductor. He was born in Lawrence, Massachusetts to a Ukrainian Jewish family. He studied at Harvard and the Curtis Institute in Philadelphia and had a remarkable debut as a conductor in 1943 when he stood in for Bruno Walter. His career as conductor took off immediately and he was in great demand, eventually becoming musical director of the New York Philharmonic in 1958. Both in his orchestral compositions and his operas and musicals, Bernstein managed to bridge the gap between the worlds of serious and popular music. He is best remembered for his Broadway – and often cinema – successes, such as *On the Town* and *West Side Story*.

DID YOU KNOW?

Bernstein was also famous for his work as an educator. His Young People's Concerts were made for CBS television in the 1950s and are still reckoned to be the most successful musical appreciation programmes ever made.

Hans Werner Henze (1926–)

Hans Werner Henze was born in Germany but moved to Italy in 1953 as he felt both his politics and his homosexuality were not tolerated in his native land. He is a Marxist and a member of the Communist Party of Italy and his convictions are clear in his music. He was influenced by Schoenberg's atonality but also by Stravinsky and jazz. His first opera, in 1949, was *Das Wunder-theater* and in 1950 *Boulevard Solitude*, a jazz version of the Manon Lescaut story, followed. His music became more lyrical after his move to

Italy and he continued writing operas, including *König Hirsch, Der Prinz von Homburg, Elegy for Young Lovers, Der junge Lord* and *The Bassarids*. He continued to write symphonies, chamber and songs and his later operas include *We Come to the River, Pollicino* (for children), *The English Catv, Das verratene Meer* and *L'Upupu und der Triumph der Sohnesliebe* (*The Hoopoe and the Triumph of Filial Love*).

Harrison Birtwistle (1934–)

Birtwistle was born in Lancashire and studied at the Royal Manchester College of Music and at the Royal Academy of Music in London. His first, highly controversial, opera appeared in 1968 at the Aldeburgh Festival. *Punch and Judy* offended many with its explicit violence and Benjamin Britten was rumoured to have left at the interval of the first performance. Nevertheless, Birtwistle proved a prolific composer of piano and orchestral works and particularly of operas. These include *The Mask of Orpheus, Gawain, The Second Mrs Kong, The Last Supper, The Io Passion* and *The Minotaur* in 2008.

Peter Maxwell Davies (1934–)

Peter Maxwell Davies was born in Manchester and studied at the Royal Manchester College of Music, meeting fellow students Harrison Birtwistle, John Ogdon, Elgar Howarth and Alexander Goehr, with whom he formed the New Music Manchester group, committed to contemporary music. In 1962 he went to Princeton University on a Harkness Fellowship where he studied with Roger Sessions, Milton Babbit and Earl Kim. Known for his uncompromising modernism, he often shocked critics and audiences with such compositions as *Eight Songs for a Mad King*. Nevertheless, he became composer in residence at the University of Adelaide in 1965. He was knighted in 1987 and appointed Master of the Queen's Music in 2004. He moved to the Orkney Islands in 1971 and runs the St Magnus summer music festival there. He was one of the first composers to open a music download site, *MaxOpus*, in 1996. His compositions include orchestral pieces, music theatre, music for dance, film and for children. He has written several operas, including *The Martyrdom of St Magnus, The Lighthouse, The Doctor of Myddfai, Mr Emmet Takes a Walk* and *Resurrection*. His operas for children include *A Selkie Tale, The Great Bank Robbery* and *The Spider's Revenge*.

Chapter 3

FIFTY OPERA LEGENDS –
ON THE STAGE

Roberto Alagna (1963–)

Alagna was born near Paris to Sicilian parents and began his musical career as a busker, switching to opera later, but has continued to be – astonishingly – mostly self-taught. He won the Luciano Pavarotti competition and his debut was as Alfredo in *La Traviata* in 1988, a role that was to become one he was particularly well known for. He went on to sing at Covent Garden, La Scala and the Metropolitan Opera. His career suffered a blip in 2006 when he walked off stage in Zeffirelli's production of *Aida* at La Scala, upset by booing in the audience. He redeemed himself in the same role at the Met in 2007, where he had a standing ovation. He married the Romanian soprano Angela Gheorghiu in 1996 but in 2009 announced they had separated, and in December that year they failed to appear together as previously announced in *Carmen* at the Met, Gheorghiu pulling out.

Thomas Allen (1944–)

Sir Thomas Boaz Allen (he was knighted in 1999) is one of England's best-loved baritones, appearing in the UK with the Welsh National Opera, Glyndebourne and Covent Garden. He made his Metropolitan Opera debut in 1981 as Papageno and is in demand internationally: Chicago, La Scala, Salzburg, and around the world. Renowned not only for a beautiful voice but his presence as an actor, he also directs opera. His famous roles include Don Giovanni, Eisenstein in *Die Fledermaus*, Rossini's Figaro, Mozart's Almaviva, Don Alfonso in *Così fan tutte*, and he created the title role for Busoni's *Doktor Faust*.

Janet Baker (1933–)

From the 1950s, Janet Baker became one of England's most famous singers, renowned for her mezzo-soprano voice, which was full of beauty and emotion. Her performance as Dido in Berlioz' *Les Troyens* for both Scottish Opera and Covent Garden was legendary. Other key roles were Marguerite in Berlioz' *Faust*, Poppea, Dorabella, Octavian in *Der Rosenkavalier*, William Walton's Cressida, Gluck's Orfeo and Donizetti's Mary Stuart. She was also an important part of the regeneration of interest in early composers such as Monteverdi, Handel and Purcell, as well as many new ones, particularly Walton and Britten. She is a great performer, was too, of lieder and oratorio. She became a Dame in 1976 and her final performance was as Orfeo at Glyndebourne in 1982.

Josephine Barstow (1940–)

Much loved, especially on the British stage, Josephine Barstow was born in Sheffield and made her professional debut as Mimi in *La Bohème* in 1964 with the touring company Opera for All. She went on to Sadler's Wells, the Welsh National Opera and made her debut at Covent Garden in 1969 as one of the nieces in *Peter Grimes*. A regular at Covent Garden, Glyndebourne and English National Opera, she has also appeared in New York, Chicago, Bayreuth and Vienna. Famous roles include Violetta in *La Traviata*, Natasha in *War and Peace*, Leonore in *Fidelio*, and in the title roles in *Lady Macbeth of Mtsensk*, *Salome*, *Aida*, *Tosca*, *Arabella* and *Der Rosenkavalier*. She created the roles of Denise in *The Knot Garden* and Gayle in *The Ice Break*, both by Tippett, and was made a Dame of the British Empire in 1995.

Teresa Berganza (1935–)

Teresa Berganza was born in Madrid and is a mezzo as noted for the warmth of her stage persona as for her musical virtuosity, particularly in Rossini and Mozart. She trained at the Madrid Conservatory and made her operatic debut as Dorabella in *Così fan tutte* in 1957 in Aix-en-Provence. Debuts at La Scala, Glyndebourne, Covent Garden and the Met soon followed. Noted roles include Carmen, Cherubino, La Cenerentola, and she has also appeared in nine films including the 1972 *Il Barbiere di Siviglia* and as Zerlina in Joseph Losey's 1979 *Don Giovanni*, as well as making appearances as a straight actress in a number of Spanish films.

Carlo Bergonzi (1924–)

Bergonzi's stylish lyric tenor is most closely associated with Verdi, though his debut was as Rossini's Figaro in 1948 – as a baritone. He was born near Parma in Italy and his musical studies were cut short by the Second World War, when he was interned in a German POW camp. His other baritone roles included Belcore in *L'Elisir d'Amore*, Silvio in *Pagliacci*, Lescaut in *Manon Lescaut* and Rigoletto. In 1951 he had his second debut – as a tenor – in the title role of *Andrea Chénier*. Thereafter he took on a number of roles, usually Verdian, that took him to starring roles in all of the world's foremost opera houses, from Chicago to London and the Met to La Scala. He has been a major recording artist particularly of operas by Verdi, Puccini, Mascagni and Leoncavallo.

Andrea Bocelli (1958–)

Bocelli is not only an operatic superstar, he's a pop star, too, and has sold seventy million albums worldwide. He was born in Tuscany where his parents had a farm and suffered from poor eyesight from birth, becoming completely blind at the age of twelve. He won a singing competition at the age of fourteen, but qualified as a lawyer, earning money by working as a piano bar singer in the evenings. His breakthrough, though, was with the Italian rock star Zucchero with whom he sang on tour in 1993, and this led on to a recording contract and his first album went platinum in Italy. Though he had been singing operatic arias, often in rock concerts, for some time, his opera debut was as Macduff in Verdi's *Macbeth* at the Teatro Verdi in Pisa. Nevertheless, he continued with other kinds of music, too, recording a single with Sarah Brightman, 'Time to Say Goodbye', which sold three million copies. His first major operatic role finally came in 1998 when he sang Rodolfo in *La Bohème* and the next year he took the US by storm, singing at the John F Kennedy Centre in Washington and then at the White House for Bill Clinton. Later the same year he performed at the Royal Variety Performance in the presence of the Queen. He undertook a world tour in 2000 and has given many performances at special events from the re-opening of the Leaning Tower of Pisa to a memorial concert at New York's Ground Zero. Critics have criticized his diction and lack of technique, but he has won many awards, particularly for his recordings, as well as being one of *People* magazine's 'fifty most beautiful people' in 1998!

James Bowman (1941–)

James Bowman has reinstated the countertenor voice almost singlehandedly on the contemporary stage. Many operas during the baroque period had leading men who were *castrati* and, as such, the principal opera stars of their day. With the revival of interest in baroque operas, these roles have often been taken by women. Bowman, however, has reintroduced modern audiences to the countertenor voice. He was born in Oxford and was a boy chorister at Ely Cathedral, and continued singing church music when he went to New College, Oxford. His first opera appearance was in Benjamin Britten's *A Midsummer Night's Dream*, playing Oberon. He was the first countertenor to appear at Glyndebourne in Cavalli's *La Calisto* and went on to perform at English National Opera, the Royal Opera, La Scala, Milan, Amsterdam, Sydney and many other leading opera houses. He has created countertenor roles in many new operas by such composers as Richard Rodney Bennett.

Grace Bumbry (1937–)

Renowned soprano Bumbry actually began as a mezzo, memorably appearing as Eboli in Visconti's production of *Don Carlos* in 1963 and before that as Venus in *Tannhäuser* in Bayreuth, a controversial casting at the time because of her colour, but the acclaim was universal and launched her career. Her debut was in 1960 as Amneris in a remarkable career that was to continue until 1997. At the age of seventeen she had won a competition, for which the prize was a scholarship to the local music conservatory. However, Bumbry was born in Missouri, where there was still segregation, and she was not allowed to attend an all-white school, so went to Boston instead. For the first part of her career she sang as a mezzo – including a notable Carmen – but later she moved towards soprano roles, such as Salome at Covent Garden in 1970, Tosca at the Met in 1971, as well as Norma, Medea and Gioconda. Her last performance was as Klytämnestra in Richard Strauss's *Elektra* in Lyon in 1997, and she has subsequently become a sought-after teacher and competition judge.

Montserrat Caballé (1933–)

Caballé was born in Barcelona and, after training at the Liceu Conservatory, went to Basel in Switzerland and then Bremen in Germany singing a wide range of roles from Puccini to Strauss to Mozart. She hit the big time in 1965 when her performance in Donizetti's *Lucrezia Borgia* was rewarded by a twenty-five-minute standing ovation. A glittering career was launched, which saw her appear in all the great opera houses, producing a long list of recordings and a particularly strong association with the bel canto roles of Donizetti, Verdi, Bellini and Rossini.

DID YOU KNOW?

The singer has two children with her husband, the tenor Bernabe Marti: a son, Bernabe, and a daughter, Montserrat (also known as 'Montsita'), who is an opera singer too, and on occasion mother and daughter have appeared together and have recorded an album of songs and arias.

Maria Callas (1923–1977)

Probably the single most famous soprano of all time, Callas was renowned equally for her vivid characterizations on stage and her turbulent life off it – her affair with Aristotle Onassis and her 'diva-ish' behaviour were legendary. One of the few sopranos to range from the bel canto operas of

Donizetti, Bellini and Rossini to classical *opera seria* and even Wagner, she was born Sophia Cecelia Kalos in New York of Greek parents. She went to live in Athens as a teenager when her parents split up. Her mother made her sing from an early age as a means of making money and Callas's relationship with her deteriorated until, as an adult, they never communicated. The voice was phenomenal from an early age and her teachers mostly taught her how to control it. Her debut in a leading role was as Tosca at the Greek National Opera in 1942, to become one of her most famous parts. She made her Italian debut in *La Gioconda* at Verona and later as Isolde – a role she bluffed her way into, saying she knew the score, which she sight-read for the audition. In Venice in 1949 she sang in the same season Brünnhilde and Elvira in *I puritani*. The critics predicted that the same soprano could not possibly accomplish this, but were completely confounded and pronounced her a miracle! Her greatest roles included Lucia di Lammermoor, Tosca, Violetta, Anna Bolena, La Sonnambula, Medea, Norma – the list is endless, and she remains one of the best-selling recording artists to this day.

DID YOU KNOW?

Callas was overweight during the first part of her career until she went on a drastic diet, which some blame for the deterioration of her voice. She had never had any confidence in her appearance and recalled:

> My sister was slim and beautiful and friendly, and my mother always preferred her. I was the ugly duckling, fat and clumsy and unpopular. It is a cruel thing to make a child feel ugly and unwanted ... I'll never forgive her for taking my childhood away. During all the years I should have been playing and growing up, I was singing or making money. Everything I did for them was mostly good and everything they did to me was mostly bad.

José Carreras (1946–)

Carreras was born in Barcelona and, during a particularly difficult time in Spain's history, he recalls his childhood as completely carefree. He was singing from the earliest age, mostly to entertain his family and friends. At the age of six he saw Mario Lanza in the film *The Great Caruso* and came home able to sing all the arias. It was inevitable he would study music and he made early appearances on Spanish radio and, at eleven, he was the boy soprano in de Falla's *El retablo de Maese Pedro*. He was encouraged by Montserrat Caballé and he sang Gennaro in Donizetti's *Lucrezia Borgia* as his official debut, and went on to sing with her frequently, including his British debut *Maria Stuarda* at the Royal Festival Hall. What was clear from the very beginning was that his was not just a beautiful lyric tenor voice, but that Carreras was also a formidable actor. In his twenties he was already hugely successful – unusually early for a tenor – and he sang at major opera houses all over the world for the next two decades, an astonishing sixty roles, until he received the devastating news in 1987 that he had acute leukaemia and had a slim chance of survival. Miraculously, he not only survived, but returned to opera. His fame spread far beyond the opera world when he became known as one of The Three Tenors with Pavarotti and Domingo. He has latterly moved into Neapolitan songs and a musical crossover with such stars as Sarah Brightman, Diana Ross and Debbie Harry, as well as becoming a prodigious fundraiser for leukaemia.

Enrico Caruso (1873–1921)

Born in Naples to a poor family, he could be seen as the first modern tenor, being a pioneer of the new recording techniques that would make him remembered long after his contemporaries were forgotten – his 'Vesti la giubba' was the first recording ever to sell a million copies. The recordings took place in the USA, where Caruso appeared at the Met more than 800 times. He left school at eleven to train as an apprentice mechanic but earned pocket money singing in the street and in bars and cafes, and at sixteen took formal singing lessons. He was soon singing on the opera stage at provincial opera houses throughout Italy, until in 1900 he got his big break, to sing Rodolfo in *La Bohème* at La Scala under the baton of Toscanini. He would soon start touring, singing everywhere from Buenos Aires to St Petersburg. Then in 1902 he made the first recordings that would become best-sellers all over the world, and which brought him engagements in London and New York. Puccini created the role of Dick Johnson in *La fanciulla del West* specifically for Caruso and he undertook a punishing schedule of performances all of his adult life. This may have been a contributing factor to his early death at forty-eight, and during his last year he suffered from a series of illnesses including bronchitis, pleurisy, migraines and emphysema. The Italian King Victor Emmanuel III opened the Royal Basilica for a funeral attended by thousands of mourners.

DID YOU KNOW?

Though New York was Caruso's second home, it wasn't always plain sailing. In 1906 he was accused of an indecent act in the monkey house of Central Park Zoo. A lady claimed he had pinched her bottom. Caruso claimed it wasn't him; it was a monkey – unsuccessfully.

Feodor Chaliapin (1873–1938)

The most famous Russian bass of all time, Chaliapin was born into a peasant family and was mostly self-taught. His remarkable voice was matched by an extraordinary stage presence and his naturalistic acting has been thought to have been the inspiration for Stanislavsky's theories on the art of acting. His career began in Russia at the Imperial Opera in St Petersburg and at the Marmontov Private Opera in Moscow, including, as Boris Godunov, the role for which he became renowned. He sang at La Scala and the Met in New York and then formed an association with Serge Diaghilev, the Russian impresario, who launched him in London and Paris. After the revolution in Russia, his career was essentially itinerant, notably in New York and London. He also made a film with GW Pabst in 1933, *The Adventures of Don Quixote*, recorded in three versions: French, English and German.

A BRAWLING SINGER

Rachmaninov recalled Chaliapin's backstage temper thus:

Feodor *is* a brawler. They are all scared of his very spirit. He shouts suddenly or even hits someone! And Feodor's fist is powerful ... He can take care of himself. And how else should one behave? Backstage at our own theatre it's just like a saloon. They shout, they drink, they swear in the foulest language.

Boris Christoff (1914–1993)

Born in Bulgaria, Christoff was a boy chorister at the Alexander Nevsky Cathedral in Sofia. He studied law and became a magistrate but at the same time was singing at the cathedral and with the city's opera as a bass. In 1942 he left Bulgaria for Italy, where he was tutored by Riccardo Stracciari, the great baritone. He gave concerts but it was not until after the war in 1946 that he made his opera debut in *La Bohème* at Reggio Calabria and later that year sang King Mark in *Tristan und Isolde*. He sang, too, in the increasingly popular Russian operas as well as Wagner, Verdi and Monteverdi. He was due to make his debut at the Met in 1950 but the US authorities had barred Eastern European citizens entry and he would only be allowed in six years later – and he was never to sing at the Met. Instead, he sang in Paris and London, Italy and Spain. A contemporary of Callas, they frequently shared a stage, though their professional relationship was to end in tears with *Medea* in Rome in 1955 when cuts were made in Christoff's role and he blocked her way to take a solo curtain call at the end of the performance. In the end no one appeared on stage to receive the applause. The theatre manager remarked, 'It's nothing serious. Just a Greco-Bulgarian war.'

DID YOU KNOW?
Christoff's brother-in-law was Tito Gobbi.

Franco Corelli (1921–2003)

Corelli's heroic tenor was particularly suited to dramatic Italian roles and his handsome and thrilling stage presence made him hugely popular in his twenty-five-year career. He became a singer almost by an accident when a friend dared him to enter a music competition. He didn't win, but he did decide to enter the conservatory in Bologna where he developed into a fine tenor with a particularly outstanding upper register. His debut in 1951 was as Don José in *Carmen* and soon after he sang Pollione in *Norma* opposite Maria Callas, a partnership that was to blossom over the next few years in a host of leading opera houses. In 1961 he went to the Met in New York and this was to be his second home for the next fourteen years, starring as Calaf, Romeo, Cavaradossi and Rodolfo, among others. He made many hugely successful recordings. He retired in 1976.

Plácido Domingo (1941–)

Plácido Domingo, one of the world-famous Three Tenors, was born in Madrid to parents who were traditional Zarzuela performers. A remarkable singer, dramatic performer and now a conductor too, he has never stopped working and has thrived on constantly pushing his own boundaries over an astonishingly versatile range of roles – in total, 124, from Wagner to Strauss, Tchaikovsky to Verdi and numerous new composers as well as some crossover into other musical styles. His parents moved to Mexico when he was eight and he studied at Mexico City's conservatory, at first focusing on piano and conducting and only gradually moving across to singing. His debut was Alfredo in *La Traviata* in Monterrey and after a two-year stint at the Israel National Opera in Tel Aviv, in 1966 he created the title role of Ginastera's *Don Rodrigo* at the New York City Opera, then moved to the Met, where he became one of the company's favourite stars (he has opened the season twenty-one times), as he has been at Covent Garden, La Scala, Teatro Colon in Buenos Aires, and just about every major opera house on the planet. His recordings have been regular bestsellers (eight have gone gold, selling over a million copies). In 1990 he appeared with Carreras and Pavarotti at the opening of the World Cup in Rome and introduced opera to a whole new audience. In 2009, while he continued to sing tenor roles, he also began to take on baritone ones, the first being the title role in *Simon Boccanegra*. He has appeared in several award-winning films including *La Traviata*, *Madama Butterfly*, *Carmen*, *Otello* and two versions of *Tosca*. Domingo has for a long time been very active in charitable work, including the José Carreras International Leukaemia Foundation, and benefit concerts after Hurricane Katrina in New Orleans and the Mexico City earthquake, and in 1993 he founded an international competition for young singers, called Operalia.

DID YOU KNOW?
Domingo thrives on work. He has famously said, 'If I rest, I rust.'

Geraint Evans (1922–1992)

Sir Geraint Llewellyn Evans was one of British opera's best-loved stars. A distinguished baritone, he had a career that lasted almost forty years and embraced a wide range of roles. He is, though, best remembered for a remarkable comic talent as Falstaff, Leporello, Figaro, Papageno and Don Pasquale, as well as a wonderful Bottom in Britten's *A Midsummer Night's Dream*. He was born in Cilfynydd in Wales and spoke Welsh before he spoke English. He had a limited education, leaving school at fourteen, but he took singing lessons and sang in an amateur capacity in the church choir and with local drama societies. During the war he was a radio mechanic but sang in service entertainments and after the war took more lessons, joined the Royal Opera House in 1948 and received his first major role a year later as Mozart's Figaro. He was one of the first British opera singers to receive international recognition, singing at La Scala, Vienna, Salzburg and at many US opera houses. He was knighted in 1969 – his autobiography is *A Knight at the Opera*.

A CHARMING SINGER

Evans is remembered with much fondness by audiences and colleagues alike. He was, though, no pushover, as Peter Ustinov remembered when he tried to direct him:

His great qualities are a permanent commentary on all that make opera inviting, and finally impossible, to someone trained in the theatre. With his fine eighteenth-century face, looking like many of the actors' portraits in the Garrick club, dark eyes, bulbous nose and chubby cheeks, on the small side, bristling with invention, ferociously energetic, helpful, greedy, understanding, and unscrupulous, he knows from the outset what he intends to do, usually because he has already done it successfully, and rehearsals are spent getting his own way by running the whole gamut of techniques, from charm to bluster and back again.

Kathleen Ferrier (1912–1953)

Ferrier was born in Lancashire, England and, while naturally musical, she had little formal education, leaving school at fourteen. She married Bert Wilson, a bank manager, in 1935, and it was he who was responsible for her singing career, daring her to compete in a music competition, which she went on to win in two categories: piano and singing. She next won the Gold Cup of 1938 at Workington Music Festival and gave concerts during the war. Her radiant contralto voice and her warm personality made her a great favourite with the public and while she was renowned for her performances in operas – notably Lucretia in Britten's *The Rape of Lucretia* and Euridice in Gluck's *Orfeo ed Euridice* – she mostly sang concert performances, which included songs by both classical composers (Bach, Brahms, Schubert and Schumann) and folk songs, mostly famously 'Blow the Wind Southerly'. Her final performance was as Euridice at Covent Garden when she already had breast cancer and it was spreading to her bones. She left the theatre on a stretcher and died later that year.

Dietrich Fischer-Dieskau (1925–)

One of the greatest baritones of the twentieth century, Fischer-Dieskau was born in Berlin and took singing lessons from the age of sixteen. Drafted into the Wehrmacht in 1943, he was captured by the Americans, and during his time as a prisoner of war he sang lieder to his fellow prisoners. In 1947 he returned to Germany and began as a professional performer, singing first lieder on the concert stage and then a year later with the Berlin Stadische Opera, later the Deutsche Oper, which would become his principal stage for the rest of his career. However, he went on to sing, too, on many other stages, including Covent Garden, Vienna, France, Switzerland, Salzburg, Japan and the US. He excelled in German operas but also in Italian and much contemporary music and made many successful recordings. Some of his most famous roles include Busoni's Dr Faust, Falstaff, Jochanaan, Onegin, Don Giovanni, Wozzeck, Amfortas, Rigoletto and Macbeth.

Renée Fleming (1959–)

Fleming was born in Pennsylvania, the daughter of two music teachers. She studied at the Crane School of Music, the New York University at Potsdam and the Juilliard School, when she was already singing professionally. Her first major role was Konstanze in *Die Entführung aus dem Serail* in Salzburg but it was two years later when she shot to fame as the Countess in *The Marriage of Figaro* with Houston Grand Opera. She has a warm, full soprano voice, which is particularly celebrated in her roles as Arabella, Violetta, the Marschallin, Rusalka, Desdemona, Lucrezia Borgia, Pamina and Donna Anna. She has made many recordings and appeared on the soundtrack to the 2003 film *The Lord of the Rings: The Return of the King* and sang at President Obama's Inauguration in 2009.

Mirella Freni (1935–)

Born Mirelli Fregni in Modena, Italy, she sang from childhood, winning a radio competition at age ten and making her operatic debut aged nineteen as Micaela in *Carmen*. She went on to Mimi in *La Bohème* and in 1960 made her debut at Glyndebourne with Adina in *L'Elisir d'Amore*, as well as Susanna in *The Marriage of Figaro* and Zerlina in *Don Giovanni*. Covent Garden, La Scala and the Met soon followed. She has a natural musicality and a youthful quality both vocally and dramatically, which made such roles as Mimi, Juliette, Nanetta in *Falstaff* and Marguerite in *Faust* particularly appropriate, though she later took on such parts as Desdemona, Leonora, Tosca and Aida. Her final performance before retirement was at the age of seventy, when she sang the teenage Joan of Arc.

DID YOU KNOW?
Mirella's mother worked alongside Pavarotti's in a cigarette factory (shades of *Carmen*)!

Angela Gheorghiu (1965–)

The glamorous Romanian soprano has been known as much for her tempestuous private life as she has for her undoubtedly fine, rich voice. Her dramatic style is equally rich and she is admired for her heart-breaking Violetta and sensuous Tosca. Born in Romania, she studied music at the university in Bucharest, graduating in 1990. Two years later she made her debut at Covent Garden as Zerlina in *Don Giovanni*. She has sung at the Vienna State Opera, the New York Met and San Francisco among others and made many extremely popular recordings, most especially with her husband, the tenor Roberto Alagna, whom she married in 1996. However, she has had volatile relationships with a number of opera houses and directors, fighting with Zeffirelli about wearing a blonde wig to play Micaela in *Carmen*, refusing to sign the contract to play Violetta opposite her husband at the Met until past the deadline (the Met hired another two singers), losing her job at Chicago's *La Bohème* for missing rehearsals and finally withdrawing from *Carmen* in December 2009 after a much-publicized break-up with her husband, who was to play opposite her again at the Met. Despite all of this, she is still in demand for her beautiful voice and dazzling appearance.

Tito Gobbi (1913–1984)

The man who would become the greatest Italian baritone of the twentieth century was studying law at the University of Padua when a family friend, who was also a musician, on hearing him sing, advised him to study opera. Fortunately, he did. Known for his musical intelligence, fine, rich baritone and powerful on-stage presence, he became a favourite at Covent Garden, Chicago, Rome, La Scala, the Met, Paris and the Vienna Staatsoper. His repertoire was immense (over 100 roles) but he was an iconic interpreter of Rigoletto, Otello, Falstaff, Iago, Wozzeck, Simon Boccanegra, Don Carlo, Scarpia, Figaro, Count Almaviva and Don Giovanni. His Scarpia opposite Callas's Tosca in Zeffirelli's 1965 Covent Garden production is generally accepted as being an interpretation that could never be bettered and, thankfully, at least part of it is still available on DVD. He appeared in twenty-six films and has left a massive legacy of recordings.

A COLOURFUL SINGER

After Gobbi's death, Sir John Tooley, director of the Royal Opera House wrote:

Tito was one of the most exceptional artists of our times … for his deep understanding of the character, the diligence in his research … the acute observation of human nature … All this was fused into a voice … that he could colour to illuminate the text and the thoughts and feelings of the character which he was both playing and living. Tito's contribution to the development of opera and to its growth as a vital and living art form is beyond doubt.

Hans Hotter (1909–2003)

Hans Hotter was probably the greatest Wagnerian bass-baritone of his age. He studied in Munich and worked as a choirmaster before his opera debut in 1930 at Troppau. He sang his first Wotan in Munich and this would prove to be the key role of his career, playing it again in Bayreuth in the early 1950s and continuing with it until almost the end of his career, when he recorded it under Georg Solti. He was a pillar of the Vienna and Munich Operas, Covent Garden and Bayreuth, mostly singing Wagnerian roles, but also the Grand Inquisitor in *Don Carlo*, Rossini's Don Basilio and Boris Godunov.

DID YOU KNOW?
Hotter was much admired by Hitler, who had some of his recordings and was believed to listen to them regularly. According to Hotter's *Times* obituary, when asked about this, Hotter replied that the Pope had some of them too.

Anne Howells (1941–)

This attractive English singer has played both mezzo-soprano roles – such as Dorabella at Covent Garden – and soprano roles – such as Poppea for Scottish Opera. She studied at the Royal Manchester College of Music from 1964–1967 and while still a student had her debut as Flora in *La Traviata* at Welsh National Opera. Debuts soon followed in Chicago, New York and Salzburg. She created the role of Lena in Richard Rodney Bennett's *Victory* in 1967 and Cathleen in Maw's *The Rising of the Moon* for Glyndebourne in 1970, and Régine in Liebermann's *La Forêt*.

Rita Hunter (1933–2001)

Rita Hunter was born in Wallasey, Merseyside and after studying singing in Liverpool and London joined the chorus of the Sadler's Wells Opera Company (later English National Opera). After studying with Eva Turner, she returned as a principal, singing dramatic roles such as Donna Anna in *Don Giovanni*, Elizabeth in *Don Carlos*, Leonora in *Il Trovatore* and, most importantly of all, the role that would define her career, Brünnhilde. She was to become a major Wagnerian in the UK, US and eventually Australia, where she settled permanently in 1981.

Gwyneth Jones (1936–)

The acclaimed Welsh dramatic soprano studied in London, Siena and Zurich and actually made her debut as a mezzo but soon changed to soprano. She shot to fame as Leonore in *Fidelio* with Welsh National Opera and in 1964 stood in for Leontyne Price as Leonora in *Il Trovatore*. After this, major roles followed, including Aida, Desdemona, Octavian, the Marschallin, Tosca, Donna Anna and Kundry in *Parsifal*. Her powerful voice and superb dramatic skill made her a natural for Wagner and she made a magnificent Brünnhilde in the centennial production of the Ring under Pierre Boulez. As well as Wagner, later core roles included Elektra, Turandot and Norma, but she also played Ruth in *The Pirates of Penzance* and Hanna Glawari in *The Merry Widow*. She became a Dame Commander of the British Empire in 1986.

Lotte Lehmann (1888–1976)

The German, later American, soprano had a massive repertoire, though she was most closely associated with German composers and was the definitive Marschallin of her age in *Der Rosenkavalier*. From 1914 to 1938 she sang with the Vienna State Opera, creating the roles of the Composer in *Ariadne auf Naxos* and the Dyer's Wife in *Die Frau ohne Schatten*. During the same period, she sang at Covent Garden, Salzburg and at the Met in New York with roles as varied as Elsa in *Lohengrin* and Mimi in *La Bohème*, Manon and Suor Angelica. She made many recordings of both opera and lieder, and taught master classes in California – she had emigrated to the US in 1938. She was also a poet and novelist and published several books.

Jenny Lind (1820–1887)

The Swedish Nightingale was the illegitimate daughter of a teacher in Stockholm and was 'discovered' by the maid of the principal dancer at the Royal Swedish Opera who heard her singing as a young child. The maid returned with her mistress, an audition was arranged and by the age of ten Jenny was singing on stage. By her late teens she was a favourite in Sweden and in her twenties started touring – including to Denmark, where Hans

Christian Andersen fell in love with her and was inspired to write *The Ugly Duckling*, *The Angel* and *The Nightingale*. She also travelled throughout Europe, to England and, eventually, America and was a triumph everywhere she went. Mendelssohn was supposedly in love with her, but after his premature death in 1847 she was too upset to sing in his oratorio, *Elijah*, in which he had written a part (including a high F sharp) for her. When she did sing it a year later, she raised £1,000 to fund the Mendelssohn Scholarship. She was so charitably generous throughout her life, in fact, that this all added to the 'Lind mania' that was rampant throughout Europe and America. She was able to fund this in part because of PT Barnum, the circus owner, who had heard of her sell-out successes and she was heavily promoted as much for her virtue as her voice. Barnum agreed to pay her the staggering sum of $1,000 for each of some 150 concerts, in spite of the fact that she was unheard of in America. The risk paid off. After marrying pianist Otto Goldschmidt, Lind had three children and eventually settled in Malvern in Worcestershire, having given up her operatic career, perhaps on the advice of a clergyman who told her the stage and God were incompatible.

Victoria de los Angeles (1923–2005)

Victoria de los Angeles was born into a poor family in Barcelona and was to become a world-famous soprano known for her deep musicality, beautiful lyric voice and her charm both on and off the stage. She studied at the

A DISARMING SINGER

Victoria de los Angeles' charisma and modesty somehow found a balance and she was self-deprecating about her own achievements, saying:

So don't think in reality I am a singer, I think I am a human being that has sung always all her life, and has learned a little to sing, and has found herself in the middle of a career.

Conservatory in Barcelona and made her professional debut as the Countess in *The Marriage of Figaro* in 1945 at the Liceu there, and then at the Paris Opera as Marguerite in 1949 and at Covent Garden as Mimi in 1950. This created a sensation. She went on to New York, Vienna, La Scala and, in 1961, Bayreuth. The roles most closely associated with her include Mimi, the Countess in *The Marriage of Figaro*, Carmen, Butterfly, Salud in Falla's *La Vida Breve*, Elsa in *Lohengrin*, Manon and Rossini's Rosina.

Benjamin Luxon (1937–)

One of the most versatile baritones of the last century, Luxon is still entertaining audiences today, often with less song and more readings, but with the inimitable style and charm intact. He was born in Cornwall and studied at the Guildhall School of Music and Drama in London. He made his name in 1970 creating the title role of Benjamin Britten's *Owen Wingrave*, though he was already a well-established member of Britten's English Opera Group. In 1972 he made his debut at Covent Garden, again creating a role, this time the Jester in Peter Maxwell Davies's opera *Taverner*. But he did not only appear in contemporary operas and other notable parts included a striking Count in *The Marriage of Figaro* at Glyndebourne, Falstaff at the English National Opera, Eugene Onegin at the Met, and Marcello in *La Bohème*. He now lives in Massachusetts where he has a new career as a narrator and poetry reader.

Maria Malibran (1808–1836)

Born in Paris to a famous Spanish musical family, she was to become its most exciting member. Thrilling both for her voice – a mezzo but with the range of a soprano – and as an incomparable actress, she was equally good in tragedy and comedy. Her early death at twenty-eight was the result of a fall from a horse and, living life at full pelt, for many she summed up the entire Romantic movement. She was remembered by such musicians as Rossini, Lamartine and Bellini as the most thrilling singer in operatic history. Her father, Manuel Garcia, was relentless in his teaching and she first appeared on stage with him at the age of eight. At the age of seventeen she made her debut as Rosina in *The Barber of Seville* first in London and then in New York. She would become New York's first prima donna, introducing the city to eight new operas. She married a banker, Francois Eugene Malibran, rather suddenly – perhaps to escape from her father. But she soon left him and returned to Europe where she conquered Paris, London, Milan and Rome, singing mostly Italian opera. Her Amina in *La Sonnambula* was an enormous success, and her Norma in Milan caused a virtual riot. Other signature roles included La Cenerentola, Semiramide, Maria Stuarda (she created the role), Juliette and Desdemona.

Nellie Melba (1861–1931)

The most famous Australian soprano of all time was born Helen Porter Mitchell – she took her name from her native city of Melbourne. Technically brilliant, her voice remained pure to the end, when she gave her farewell performance at Covent Garden in 1926. But it took her some time to get there. At twenty-one, she married the seemingly glamorous Charles Nisbett Frederick Armstrong, the younger son of a baronet. But the marriage was not glamorous; they were living in a small town, Mackay, in a tin-roofed house and she wanted to sing professionally. So she went to Melbourne, trained with Pietro Cecchi and had some success, and so set off for London to try her luck there. She was not encouraged by the response – Sir Arthur Sullivan turned her down – and she decided to go to Paris instead, where she met the singer Mathilde Marchesi who coached her not just in singing but in social skills, and for this Melba was forever indebted. It paid off. In 1887 Melba made her debut in Brussels as Gilda in *Rigoletto* and was an immediate success, going on to *La Traviata* and *Lucia di Lammermoor*. She returned to Covent Garden and though she sang both Gilda and Lucia had little success, until she met Lady de Grey, who worked on her behalf to get Melba another chance. That happened in 1889 when she played Juliette. She was launched not only on to the world opera stage but, courtesy of Lady de Grey, into society. She sang at Covent Garden, La Scala and the Met and also in the homes of royalty, including Tsar Alexander III, Emperor Franz Joseph and Queen Victoria. In 1890, Melba met Philippe, Duke of Bourbon and pretender to the French throne. The two were seen together in various capital cities and, most disastrously, in a box at the opera in Vienna. Melba's husband filed for divorce, the Duke disappeared to Africa for an extended safari and Melba was left alone. Her career did not, however, falter. She went on tour to Australia and New Zealand, returned to Covent Garden and created the title role of *Hélène* in Monte Carlo. Other great roles included Mimi, Nedda in *Pagliacci*, Violetta, Rosina, Lakmé, Desdemona, Marguerite and Aida.

Birgit Nilsson (1918–2005)

Nilsson's powerful dramatic soprano made her a formidable Isolde and Brünnhilde. Besides Wagner, her voice was perfect, too, for such roles as Lady Macbeth, Aida, Donna Anna, Tosca, Salome, Electra in *Idomeneo* and the title role in *Turandot*. She was born and studied in Sweden, making her debut at Stockholm's Royal Opera in 1946, and spent much of her early career there, though she soon won international prominence appearing in Vienna, Bayreuth, Glyndebourne, Covent Garden, Buenos Aires, Sydney and, perhaps above all, New York's Metropolitan, where she became America's leading Wagnerian soprano.

A COMIC SOPRANO

Birgit Nilsson's stage presence was usually serious and dramatic. In contrast, off stage she was known for her dry sense of humour. Asked what she needed most to sing the taxing role of Isolde, she replied, 'A comfortable pair of shoes.'

Luciano Pavarotti (1935–2007)

Probably the most famous tenor of his generation, Pavarotti's big voice had famously stunning top notes and he became a household name when he sang 'Nessum dorma' from Puccini's *Turandot* at the 1990 World Cup. Born in Modena, northern Italy, Pavarotti's first ambition was to *be* a footballer, but he began studying music, discovering he had perfect pitch. However, success came slowly, beginning with local opera houses in Italy. His debut was as Rodolfo in *La Bohème* in Reggio Emilia and in 1963 he reprised the role in both Vienna and London, Covent Garden. He was soon in demand from the US to Salzburg and Vienna to La Scala, he became popular on television and his recordings went gold and platinum. He set up his International Voice Competition for young singers, performing with them in excerpts from popular operas, and gave the first ever concert in Beijing's Great Hall of the People in front of an audience of 10,000. While Pavarotti was the darling of the world's great opera houses, he was equally at home with mass audiences, from London's Hyde Park to the World Cup. He crossed over into the world of pop, too, and everywhere became accustomed to long-standing ovations – he holds the record in the *Guinness Book of Records* for the most curtain calls in one evening! He died of cancer at the age of seventy-one and, after his funeral in Modena Cathedral, was buried with his parents, the event being broadcast on CNN. Compared to the other two tenors – Domingo and Carreras – Pavarotti had a narrow repertoire, his voice being perfect for Italian bel canto roles and he rarely strayed from these. His greatest legacy of all, though, must be the bringing of opera to a vast public who would otherwise never have heard it.

DID YOU KNOW?
Pavarotti's signature white handkerchief was the result of a concert he gave in Missouri in 1973 – he had a bad cold at the time.

Peter Pears (1910–1986)

Peter Pears was the partner of the composer Benjamin Britten and the creator of many of his roles, usually composed with Pears' voice specifically in the composer's mind. Born in Hampshire, he studied music both at Keble College, Oxford and the Royal College of Music. He met Britten in 1936 and the two began giving concerts together but left Britain soon after as conscientious objectors during the war. He performed at the Met and Covent Garden but is best known for his Britten roles, including Aschenbach in *Death in Venice*, Macheath in *The Beggar's Opera*, Captain Vere in *Billy Budd*, Quint in *The Turn of the Screw*, Flute in *A Midsummer Night's Dream*, Essex in *Gloriana*, Sir Philip in *Owen Wingrave* and the title roles in *Peter Grimes* and *Albert Herring*. He originally conceived the idea of the Aldeburgh Festival, which he was to run with Britten to great acclaim, and which is a tribute to them both to this day.

Leontyne Price (1927–)

Mary Violet Leontyne Price was born in Mississippi during segregation but nevertheless rose to fame after studying music at the all-black Wilberforce College in Ohio, then the Juilliard School in New York. Her big break came in 1952 as Bess in *Porgy and Bess*, touring both the US and Europe. She sang Tosca on NBC television and then went to La Scala to sing Salome with the conductor Herbert von Karajan. Aida and Pamina followed and she became the first black American to be a New York Met prima donna. Her signature roles included Liu in *Turandot*, Donna Anna, Carmen, Butterfly, Pamina, Fiordiligi in *Così fan tutte* and Tatyana in *Eugene Onegin*, and she was the creator of Cleopatra in Barber's *Antony and Cleopatra* at the opening of the new Met in the Lincoln Center in 1966.

Margaret Price (1941–)

Born in Monmouthshire in Wales, Margaret Price was encouraged by her music teacher at school to study at the Trinity College of Music. Her debut in 1962 was as Cherubino in *The Marriage of Figaro* and it was Mozart with which her rich, creamy voice would become particularly associated. Her Mozart signature roles include Donna Anna, Fiordiligi, the Contessa and Pamina, but she was also famed for her Ariadne in Strauss's *Ariadne auf Naxos* and in Verdi's *Un ballo in maschera* and *Otello*. Her charming Mozart portraits in particular made her a favourite at Covent Garden, the Metropolitan Opera, Cologne and Vienna. She was made a Dame Commander of the Order of the British Empire in 1993.

Ruggiero Raimondi (1941–)

Born in Bologna, Italy, Raimondi was to become his country's leading bass. With his rich voice and glamorous looks he became a favourite not only on the opera stage but on film and television too. He was renowned for his Don Giovanni, Timur in *Turandot*, as Massenet's Don Quichotte, Mozart's Count Almaviva, Boris Godunov, Attila and Scarpia. His career – and his mature voice – started early and he trained at the Giuseppe Verdi Conservatory in Milan. He won the Spoleto competition for young opera singers and was soon appearing in major roles in Italian opera houses with his La Scala debut as Timur in 1968. Paris, Covent Garden, the Met and Salzburg debuts followed, as did numerous film and television appearances. In 2008 Raimondi played an Italian opera singer in the French mini-series *Les Sanglot des Anges*.

Katia Ricciarelli (1946–)

Ricciarelli was born into a poor family in the region of Venice and struggled financially to get a musical education at the Conservatory there. She had a warm, lyric soprano voice and a captivating on-stage (and on-screen) presence that was to make her a fine Anna Bolena, Mimi, Giulietta, Suor Angelica, Luisa Miller, Tosca, Aida and Elena in *La donna del lago*. Her rise to fame came soon after graduation, especially after she went on to win first the Parma Verdi and then the Voce Verdiane competitions. She was Desdemona in Franco Zeffirelli's film of *Otello* in 1986 and made numerous recordings. Towards the end of her career her voice lost its radiance and this was widely blamed on being encouraged to sing roles – such as Turandot and Desdemona – that were too vocally demanding and simply inappropriate for it.

Elisabeth Schumann (1888–1952)

Elisabeth Schumann was born in Merseburg, Germany and trained in Berlin and Dresden, making her debut in Hamburg in 1909, as the Shepherd in Wagner's *Tannhäuser*. Her infectious charm and stage personality together with her liquid, silvery voice endeared her to audiences in Germany, England, New York and Vienna, where she excelled as Zerlina in *Don Giovanni*, Susanna in *The Marriage of Figaro*, Eva in *Die Meistersinger*, Blondchen in *The Abduction from the Seraglio* and Sophie in *Der Rosenkavalier*, a role she made very much her own. She left Europe on the eve of war and settled in America to teach at the Curtis Institute of Music in Philadelphia.

Elisabeth Schwarzkopf (1915–2006)

Renowned for her beauty as well as her glorious lyric soprano, Schwarzkopf was born in Jarotschin in what was then Prussia and is now Poland. She trained in Berlin and it was here and in Vienna that she made her name during the Second World War as Konstanze in Mozart's *The Escape from the Seraglio*, Susanna in *The Marriage of Figaro*, as Mimi and Musetta in *La Bohème* and as Violetta in *La Traviata*. During this period she became a member of the Nazi Party and was therefore banned from appearing in the US for several years after the war. Post-war, she sang at the Vienna State Opera, La Scala and Covent Garden, where she was a notable Countess in *The Marriage of Figaro*. Other signature roles included Pamina, Butterfly, Sophie and later the Marschallin in *Der Rosenkavalier*, Donna Elvira in *Don Giovanni*, Madeleine in Strauss's *Capriccio*, Fiordiligi in *Così fan tutte*, Alice Ford in *Falstaff*, and she created the role of Anne Trulove in *The Rake's Progress* in 1951. She married Walter Legge, the British founder of the Philharmonia, and became British by marriage and was made a Dame in 1992. She died, aged ninety, in her sleep.

DID YOU KNOW?

When Schwarzkopf was invited on to the BBC Radio 4 programme *Desert Island Discs* and chose the eight recordings she would take with her to while away the time should she ever be shipwrecked, she chose seven that she had made herself.

Renata Scotto (1934–)

Scotto was born in Savona in Italy and became a star both for her obvious musicality and her ability as an actor from an early age. She made her debut as Violetta in Milan at just eighteen, one of the roles that she was to make her own along with Butterfly, Manon, Adina, Amina in *La Sonnambula*, Giulietta, Lucia in *Lucia di Lammermoor* and Leonora in *Il Trovatore*. She became internationally popular, appearing regularly in New York, Chicago, London, Venice, Buenos Aires, Berlin, Rome, Paris, Madrid, Tokyo and Florence, as well as making numerous recordings. She has, since the 1990s, also become an opera director for companies all over the US.

John Shirley-Quirk (1931–)

A fine actor–singer, John Shirley-Quirk was born in Liverpool and studied chemistry and physics at his local university, but also took voice lessons at the same time. In 1961 he made his debut as the Doctor at Glyndebourne in Debussy's *Pelléas et Mélisande* and his signature roles include the Count in *The Marriage of Figaro*, Don Alfonso in *Così fan tutte* and he is particularly associated with the work of Benjamin Britten, singing among other roles Coyle in *Owen Wingrave* with the English Opera Group, of which he was a leading member. He created roles in all of Britten's last five operas and that of Lev in Tippett's *The Ice Break*. He has appeared at Covent Garden, La Scala, the Met and other major opera houses and has also been a frequent concert performer around the world as a recording artist. He was made a CBE in 1975.

Joan Sutherland (1926–2010)

Joan Sutherland was born in Sydney, Australia and only started to study singing seriously at the age of eighteen. Her debut was in Sydney as Dido, after which she went to study at London's Royal College of Music, and her London debut was as the First Lady in *The Magic Flute* at Covent Garden in 1952. Early roles included Jennifer in Tippett's *Midsummer Marriage*, Gilda in *Rigoletto* and an astonishing performance as the Israelite Woman in Handel's *Samson*. It was, however, Lucia that was to make her a superstar overnight. She was nicknamed *La Stupenda* for her dazzling and seemingly effortless coloratura joined with her considerable acting abilities. She went on to triumph at the Met, Paris, La Scala and around the world, including in her native Australia. She became renowned as Norma, Elvira, Violetta, the Daughter of the Regiment, Maria Stuarda, Lucrezia Borgia and Anna Bolena. She retired in 1990 and wrote her autobiography, *A Prima Donna's Progress*, published in 1997. She became a Dame in 1979.

DID YOU KNOW?
Dame Joan's farewell appearance on the opera stage was as a guest performer at Covent Garden on a New Year's Eve *Die Fledermaus*, when she sang duets with Luciano Pavarotti and Marilyn Horne, as well as her favourite encore, 'Home, Sweet Home'.

Robert Tear (1939–)

Born in Glamorgan in Wales, Robert Tear became a choral scholar at King's College, Cambridge at the age of eighteen, but soon embarked on a solo career. He joined the English Opera Group in 1964 and played the lead in many of Britten's operas, including Quint in *The Turn of the Screw* on tours in England and Russia. He appears regularly at Covent Garden as well as giving concert performances, including Britten's *War Requiem*, *The Dream of Gerontius* and Mahler's *Das Lied von der Erde*. Some of his most renowned opera roles include Aschenbach, Dov in Tippett's *The Knot Garden*, Lensky in *Eugene Onegin* and Admetus in *Alceste*. He is increasingly in demand as both a conductor and as a narrator.

Kiri Te Kanawa (1944–)

Kiri Te Kanawa was born in Gisborne in New Zealand of mixed European and Maori ancestry. In her teens she was a pop star in New Zealand, though she was training as an opera singer at her school, Saint Mary's College in Auckland. After winning a singing competition in 1965 with an aria from *Tosca* she went to study in London at the London Opera Centre. By 1968 she was taking on minor roles but she was catapulted to fame as the Countess in *The Marriage of Figaro* under the baton of Sir Colin Davis. This led to a contract with Covent Garden and appearances all over the world, one of the first as the Countess again at the Santa Fe Opera, where another 'unknown', Frederica von Stade, played Cherubino. Debuts followed in New York, Glyndebourne, Paris, Chicago, Sydney, Vienna, San Francisco and La Scala. Her rich, vibrant and seemingly effortless soprano is a winning combination with her charismatic beauty and her most important roles include Mozart's Countess, Arabella, the Marschallin, Micaela, Desdemona, Pamina, Fiordiligi, Gounod's Marguerite, Violetta and Mimi, and she has made numerous award-winning recordings of opera and also lighter music, such as *South Pacific* and *West Side Story*, as well as Maori songs. In 1981 she sang at the wedding of Prince Charles and Lady Diana Spencer and was made a Dame in 1982.

Eva Turner (1892–1990)

Born in Oldham in the north of England, Eva Turner studied at the Royal Academy of Music in London and started her career with the Carl Rosa Opera Company, where she at first sang smaller roles, but soon worked her way up to Aida, Tosca, Butterfly and Leonora. At the age of twenty-two she made her La Scala debut under Toscanini as Freia and Sieglinde and her strong, dazzling soprano voice made her a star. She was renowned, too, as Isolde, but it was above all her Turandot for which she was famous – many say she was the best Turandot of all time. She retired in 1948 and began a new profession as a teacher of singing at the University of Oklahoma and the Royal Academy of Music in London. She was made a Dame in 1962 and though most of her recordings were made in the 1920s and 1930s they are now available as CDs. She died aged ninety-eight in 1990.

Frederica von Stade (1945–)

The American mezzo-soprano – known to her friends as 'Flicka' – was born in New Jersey and went to the Mannes College of Music in New York. She made her debut at the Met in 1970 and a year later appeared at the Santa Fe Opera as Cherubino in *The Marriage of Figaro* with Kiri te Kanawa playing the Countess. Between them, they stole the show. Her warm bel canto style has endeared her not only to opera lovers but as a crossover artist in more popular genres, and she is a frequent performer on television, especially in the United States. She has sung in opera houses around the world but her musical home is the Metropolitan Opera in New York. Favourite roles include Rossini's *La cenerentola* and Bellini's *La Sonnambula*, Berlioz' Marguerite, Strauss's Octavian and a Merry Widow. She is also a fine concert performer of such works as Canteloube's *Les chants d'Auvergne*, Ravel's *Scheherzade* and Berlioz' *Les nuits d'été* as well as a musical theatre star of *Show Boat* and *The Sound of Music*.

AN ECSTATIC SINGER

In *New York Newsday*, Frederica von Stade was eulogized thus:

Von Stade can do no wrong. Her singing was polished yet warm, like china under whose thin glaze are painted scenes of extraordinary delicacy. One heard dainty, loving anticipation and the solitary soul. It was something close to ecstasy.

Chapter 4

THIRTY OPERA LEGENDS – IN THE PIT AND BEHIND THE SCENES

Claudio Abbado (1933–)

Born in Milan, Abbado's first teacher was his father, violinist and composer Michelangelo Abbado. He went on to study at the Milan Conservatory and the Vienna Academy of Music. He made his debut at La Scala in 1960 and became its music director from 1968 until 1986. He is profoundly serious in his approach to music but his manner with musicians and singers is calm and intuitive. In 1986 he became music director for the Vienna State Opera, a role he held until 1991, and was also principal conductor of the London Symphony Orchestra from 1979 to 1987. He conducted, too, with the Chicago Symphony Orchestra from 1982 to 1986. In 1989 he succeeded Herbert von Karajan as chief conductor of the Berlin Philharmonic Orchestra. As an opera conductor, Abbado has given memorable interpretations of many well-known scores, such as Bellini's *I Capuleti ed I Montecchi, Don Carlos, Simon Boccanegra, Il Barbiere di Siviglia, Boris Godunov, Aida, Khovanschchina, Il viaggio a Reims* and the work of many contemporary composers such as Berg, Stockhausen and Thomas Adler. He founded the contemporary music festival Wein Modern in 1988 and the European Union Youth Orchestra in 1978.

DID YOU KNOW?
Claudio Abbado decided he wanted to become a conductor when he went to hear a concert of Debussy's Nocturnes as a young child.

John Barbirolli (1899–1970)

Born in London of Italian parents, Giovanni Battista Barbirolli was to become a much-loved if controversial conductor with a decidedly romantic style. He studied at the Trinity College of Music and the Royal College of Music and was a fine concert cellist. It was not until the First World War that he had the opportunity to conduct some fellow soldier-musicians in the Suffolk Regiment. In the early years of his professional conducting life, he conducted mostly opera, and later he divided his time between opera and orchestral music. He famously worked with the Hallé Orchestra throughout his career but he also conducted the British National Opera Company and at Covent Garden before the Second World War, specializing in Italian operas and Wagner – he conducted Eva Turner's legendary Turandot. In 1936 he was one of several guest conductors of the New York Philharmonic Orchestra, whose musicians so liked him they made him their music director for the next three years. After the war he conducted *Aida* in Vienna and returned to Covent Garden too, where he was invited to become the musical director, but, while he conducted six operas there in the fifties, he turned the job itself down. As well as concert work he conducted at the Rome Opera House and the Vienna State Opera. In 1960 he took over from Leopold Stokowski as chief conductor of the Houston Symphony Orchestra and conducted the Berlin Philharmonic Orchestra regularly. Barbirolli was knighted in 1949.

DID YOU KNOW?

During the Second World War, Barbirolli was asked by the actor Leslie Howard to swap flights on a trans-Atlantic crossing. Barbirolli landed safely but Leslie Howard's plane was shot down.

Thomas Beecham (1879–1961)

Sir Thomas Beecham was and remains a legend – wit, operatic pioneer, shameless self-publicist and self-taught conductor. He was born in St Helen's, Lancashire to a family whose wealth had been created by his grandfather's Beecham's Pills factory. He studied musical composition, largely against his family's wishes, with Charles Wood and Moritz Moszkowski but he didn't feel he was good enough to be a successful composer and turned to conducting. His professional debut was conducting Balfe's *The Bohemian Girl* at the Shakespeare Theatre in Clapham, London. In his early years conducting first the New Symphony Orchestra and then the Beecham Symphony Orchestra, he completely disregarded current public tastes and produced programmes of unknown composers such as Delius, Lalo and Smetana. As a result he lost money, but from 1910, reconciled with his father after something of a family feud, he was subsidized and started to produce operas at Covent Garden and elsewhere. In that year alone, he mounted thirty-four operas, many of them new to London and often, from the point of view of the audiences, rather obscure. He became a major figure when he gave two extraordinary premieres – Strauss's *Elektra* and *Salome*. The following year he became involved with Diaghilev's *Ballets Russes*. In 1913 he gave the British premieres of *Der Rosenkavalier*, *Boris Godunov*, *Khovanshchina* and *Ivan the Terrible*. In the 1930s he took over Covent Garden, both music and management, and conducted in Germany before the war and in the US during it. He conducted, amongst others, at the Met *Carmen*, *Manon*, *Faust* and *The Tales*

AN ABSENT-MINDED CONDUCTOR

Beecham was famed for his wit and a book of his bons mots, *Beecham Stories*, was brought out in 1978. They include such gems as:

Beecham met a lady whom he recognised, though he couldn't quite place her. He prevaricated, hoping he would remember who she was. He asked after her health.

'Oh, very well,' she replied, 'but my brother has been rather ill lately.'

'Ah yes, your brother,' responded Beecham. 'I'm sorry to hear that. And what is he doing at the moment?'

'Well, he's still king,' replied Princess Mary.

of Hoffman. After the war he returned to Britain and founded the Royal Philharmonic Orchestra, taking it on a tour of the US, Canada and South Africa in 1950. In 1958 he conducted for a season at the Buenos Aires opera house, Teatro Colón, *Otello*, *Carmen*, *Fidelio*, *The Magic Flute* and *Samson and Delilah*. He continued conducting after this, but only concerts – his opera days were over. He died aged eighty-one, having been knighted in 1916 and having succeeded to his father's baronetcy later in the same year.

Karl Böhm (1894–1981)

Böhm was born in Graz in Austria, where he was a law student, but he decided it was not the law that was to be his life's work, but music. He studied music at the Conservatory in Graz and was accepted as a conductor at the Bavarian State Opera by Bruno Walter in 1921. During the war he became music director at the Vienna State Opera. It was not until 1957 that he made his debut at the Metropolitan Opera in New York, conducting *Don Giovanni*, and it was his interpretations of Mozart, together with Strauss, that were to become particularly renowned. He gave the world premieres of Strauss's *Die Schweigsame Frau* (*The Silent Woman*) and *Daphne* (the latter is dedicated to him) in Dresden in 1935 and 1938 respectively. In New York he gave the premieres of *Ariadne auf Naxos* and *Die Frau ohne Schatten*. He was also an acclaimed conductor of Wagner, giving the entire Ring Cycle at Bayreuth is 1966 and 1967, as well as *Tristan und Isolde*. He was closely associated with the London Symphony Orchestra and held the title of its president until his death, as well as with the Vienna Philharmonic and the Salzburg Festival.

Arrigo Boito (1842–1918)

Born in Padua, Boito was a man of many parts – poet, novelist and composer – but above all he was a librettist. His own operas, *Mefistofele* and *Nerone*, were not successes, nor did they have particularly good librettos. However, he wrote the libretto for Ponchielli's *La Gioconda* under the pseudonym Tobia Gorrio – an anagram of his own name – and from there went on to write the librettos for Verdi's operas *Simon Boccanegra* and the Shakespearean operas *Otello* and *Falstaff*.

Pierre Boulez (1925–)

Born in Montbrison in France, Pierre Boulez was a student of mathematics before he was one of music at the Paris Conservatory under the tutelage of Olivier Messiaen and René Leibowitz. He composed using the twelve-tone technique and later in integral serialism and was generally involved in musical experimentation. As composer, conductor and teacher, he has been a pioneer, especially in bringing contemporary music to an often-sceptical public. *Le Marteau sans maitre* (*The Hammer without a Master*), composed in 1955, was influenced by many musical genres from jazz to African but was described both as 'a totally serial lollipop' and 'an inexpert gamelan orchestra'. His conducting career began in Baden-Baden in 1958, though he describes himself as 'allergic to opera houses'. Nevertheless, he conducted a magnificent *Parsifal* at Bayreuth in 1966 and *Pelléas et Mélisande* at Covent Garden two years later. In 1976 he was the music director of the hundredth anniversary Ring at Bayreuth, returning to conduct the next four festivals. He was also a principal conductor of the BBC Symphony Orchestra and the New York Philharmonic and, later in his career, returned to the Berliner Philharmoniker. He has made numerous recordings, mostly for Deutsche Grammophon, and conducted all over the world, including the 'Boulez 2000' tour with the London Symphony Orchestra. In 2005 Deutsche Grammophon celebrated his eightieth birthday with a range of new releases including Anne Sofie von Otter and the Wiener Philharmoniker playing Mahler, the Bartók piano concertos and his own compositions. At the time of writing, now well into his eighties, Boulez continues to compose and conduct. He is particularly renowned for his championing and interpretations of Berg (he conducted the first production of the complete *Lulu* at the Paris Opera), Debussy, Schoenberg, Stravinsky, Webern and Mahler, as well as Wagner and Berlioz. He famously dislikes Italian composers.

DID YOU KNOW?
Boulez never used a baton, preferring to conduct with his hands alone.

Hans von Bülow (1830–1894)

Von Bülow was born in Dresden and there is a possibly apocryphal story that he gave up his study of the law after hearing the premiere of *Lohengrin* under Liszt and decided to take up music instead. He did, however, study with both Wagner and Liszt, marrying Cosima, the latter's daughter, only to lose her to Wagner twelve years later. He never, though, gave up his championship of Wagner's music. Before Cosima left him in 1869 he had conducted the premiere of *Tristan und Isolde* in 1865 and *Die Meistersinger von Nürnberg* in 1868 at the Royal Opera in Munich. He then went both to Britain and the US to conduct, returning to Germany in 1878 as conductor at Hanover, and later Meiningen, Hamburg and Berlin. He was a great Wagnerian and the first truly virtuoso conductor with fine interpretation skills. He was also a superb pianist and a composer himself – usually of orchestral music – and wrote the piano arrangements of *Tristan*.

DID YOU KNOW?
Von Bülow was known for his sharp tongue, declaring 'A tenor is not a man but a disease' and 'The three greatest composers are Bach, Beethoven and Brahms. All the others are cretins.'

Colin Davis (1927–)

Born in Weybridge in Surrey, Colin Davis was in his early teens when he decided he wanted to be a musician. Educated at Christ's Hospital, he won a scholarship to the Royal College of Music, where he studied clarinet and decided he really wanted to conduct. He formed the Kalmar Orchestra with friends from the college and conducted the new Chelsea Opera Group in *Don Giovanni*. In 1957 he became assistant conductor with the BBC Scottish Orchestra but it was when he stood in for Otto Klemperer at a performance of *Don Giovanni* at Covent Garden that he started to receive real recognition. A year later he conducted *The Magic Flute* at Glyndebourne when Beecham fell ill and critical and public acclaim followed. In 1960 he became chief conductor and later musical director of Sadler's Wells Opera, where he not only had great successes with the more familiar – *Idomeneo* and *Fidelio* – but introduced the British public to the unfamiliar Weill's *Mahagonny*. In 1970 Davis became principal conductor at the Royal Opera, Covent Garden where he worked with Peter Hall as stage director before he left for the Royal Shakespeare Company, producing, among others, the premiere of Tippett's *The Knot Garden*. He became famed for his Mozart and Berlioz productions but also introduced newer operas, including Berg's *Lulu* and *Wozzeck* as well as Tippett's *The Ice Break*, which is dedicated to Davis. He took the company to La Scala in 1976 and in 1977 became the first English conductor to appear at Bayreuth with *Tannhäuser*. He conducted, too, at the Met in New York and the Vienna State Opera. He conducted a number of prominent symphony orchestras including the BBC Symphony, New York Philharmonic and London Symphony Orchestras and was the mainstay of the Proms after the departure of Sir Malcolm Sargent. He was knighted in 1980 and is still conducting in his eighties.

Sergei Diaghilev (1872–1929)

Sergei Pavlovich Diaghilev was born in Novgorod, Russia and went to St Petersburg University to study law. At the same time he studied music – though his teacher, Rimsky-Korsakov told him he had no talent. He became involved with a group of artists including Alexandre Benois and Léon Bakst and in 1899 became assistant to Prince Sergei Milhailovitch Vokonsky, who ran the Imperial Theatres. Diaghilev was soon producing plays and ballets. He left the job in 1901 in disgrace, though it is not clear why, but he turned his hand to putting on exhibitions, eventually taking one to Paris where he produced concerts and, in 1908, *Boris Godunov* at the Paris Opera, starring Feodor Chaliapin. This created a sensation and he returned the following year with operas and ballets with his new company, the *Ballets Russes*, including Anna Pavlova, Vaslav Nijinsky and Tamara Karsavina. Operas included Rimsky-Korsakov's *The Maid of Pskov, May Night* and *The Golden Cockerel*. But it was the ballet that was to cause the greatest sensation, with not only dazzling dancers, but music commissioned from such composers as Debussy, Ravel, Poulenc and Prokofiev, with Léon Bakst as artistic director producing ever more sumptuous feasts for the eye. By the 1920s, Diaghilev's star had waned, but he was singlehandedly responsible for introducing Russian opera and re-introducing classical ballet to the west.

Wilhelm Furtwängler (1886–1954)

A supreme Wagnerian conductor and acknowledged as one of the greatest conductors of the last century – and, according to many critics, the greatest conductor ever – Furtwängler made his name in Berlin and Paris in the 1920s and in the 1930s at Bayreuth and Covent Garden. He had a unique and unorthodox conducting style that seemed awkward to many and varied between trance-like states and excitable fits! However, his performances and interpretations were legendary and some are still available as recordings, such as his *Tristan und Isolde* and Ring Cycles. Controversy always hung over his career in Nazi Germany. He never joined the party and always refused to give the Nazi salute, but he was highly regarded nonetheless. He conducted at a Wagnerian concert for Hitler's birthday but towards the end of the war fled to Switzerland. He went to court after the war to defend himself against the charge of supporting Nazism by staying in Germany and conducting for most of the war, and was acquitted, though he was never allowed to conduct in the US. He said in his own defence:

I knew Germany was in a terrible crisis; I felt responsible for German music, and it was my task to survive this crisis, as much as I could. The concern that my art was misused for propaganda had to yield to the greater concern that German music be preserved, that music be given to the German people by its own musicians. These people, the compatriots of Bach and Beethoven, of Mozart and Schubert, still had to go on living under the control of a regime obsessed with total war. No one who did not live here himself in those days can possibly judge what it was like. Does Thomas Mann [who was critical of Furtwängler's actions] really believe that in 'the Germany of Himmler' one should not be permitted to play Beethoven? Could he not realize that people never needed more, never yearned more to hear Beethoven and his message of freedom and human love, than precisely these Germans, who had to live under Himmler's terror? I do not regret having stayed with them.

(Quoted from John Ardoin's *The Furtwängler Record*)

Valery Gergiev (1953–)

Gergiev was born in Moscow, but his parents returned to their native North Ossetia in the Caucasus, where he was brought up. He studied at the Conservatory in St Petersburg and in 1978 became assistant conductor at the Kirov Opera, making his debut with Prokofiev's *War and Peace*. He was chief conductor of the American Symphony Orchestra from 1981 to 1985 and went on to conduct at the Bavarian State Opera and the San Francisco Opera. In 1988 he became chief conductor and artistic director of the Mariinsky Theatre and is known around the world for his conducting of Russian operas. He is the artistic director of the White Nights Festival in St Petersburg and principal guest conductor at the Met in New York. He is much in demand as a recording artist and his recordings of Russian operas and symphonic works are particularly celebrated, especially the works of Glinka, Mussorgsky, Prokofiev, Shostakovich and Tchaikovsky.

Reginald Goodall (1901–1990)

Born in Lincoln, Goodall was to become perhaps the greatest English interpreter of Wagner, though his success came relatively late. He trained at the Royal College of Music and in 1944 he joined the Sadler's Wells Opera, later to become the English National Opera company, conducting the premiere of Britten's *Peter Grimes* the following year to great acclaim. He spent most of his career between Sadler's Wells and the Royal Opera House, Covent Garden with occasional forays to Glyndebourne. Somewhat overshadowed by Georg Solti, who was his contemporary, it was not until the sixties that he began conducting Wagner widely, becoming generally acknowledged as a great Wagnerian, noted for the poetry and majesty of his interpretations. His final performance at the Royal Albert Hall in 1987 was the third act of *Parsifal* with the English National Opera.

Tyrone Guthrie (1900–1971)

Best known as a theatre director, Tyrone Guthrie was the cousin of the actor Tyrone Power and was obsessed with the theatre from an early age. He was involved in student theatre when he was at Oxford and went on to work for the Oxford Playhouse, the BBC and in Canada, where he was director of the Shakespeare Repertory Company. He founded the Stratford Festival of Canada and the Guthrie Theater in Minneapolis. It was in the 1940s that he began producing opera, starting with *The Marriage of Figaro*, *La Bohème* and *Carmen* at Sadler's Wells in London and the Metropolitan Opera in New York, regarded by many at the time as exciting – or rather startling, depending on the point of view. He staged *Peter Grimes* at Covent Garden in 1947 and *La Traviata* at the Met in the fifties. He was a towering figure, often cavalier with both Shakespeare and opera, but one of the most important people in the moulding of Britain's classic theatre and opera companies.

WS Gilbert (1836–1911)

Sir William Schwenck Gilbert is probably the most famous librettist of all time and certainly the only librettist to feature with equal billing as the composer. The fourteen comic operas he wrote with Sir Arthur Sullivan were renowned as much for their music as the wit and charm of their words, some of which have become catchphrases to this day: 'Let the punishment fit the crime,' or 'A policeman's lot is not a happy one.' His flair for both writing and producing plays started early – at school – but his first professional production came in 1863 with his play *Uncle Baby*. He wrote in all more than seventy-five straight plays, but it was his collaboration with Arthur Sullivan that was to bring him his greatest success. They first worked together in 1871 on *Thespis, Or The Gods Grown Old*, but while this did well during the Christmas holidays at London's Gaiety Theatre there was to be a four-year gap before the pair were reunited for *Trial by Jury*, composed in a few weeks but a huge success. The Comedy Opera Company, renamed the D'Oyly Carte Opera Company, was formed in 1877 and successes soon followed: *HMS Pinafore*, *The Pirates of Penzance*, *Patience*, *Iolanthe*, *Princess Ida*, *The Mikado*, *Ruggidore*, *The Yeomen of the Guard* and

The Gondoliers. In spite of their success, the relationship was difficult, and Sullivan decided Gilbert's plots were too stylized and repetitive for him, as he really wanted to write altogether grander operas. Gilbert stopped writing operas and returned to writing plays, as well as building the Garrick Theatre.

Peter Hall (1930–)

Though generally known as a theatre director and the founder of the Royal Shakespeare Company, Peter Hall has also been an opera director of great insight and power. In 1971 he almost became Director of Productions at the Royal Opera House, Covent Garden but it was not to be and his opera work has been spasmodic, but often brilliant nonetheless. His first opera production was Gardner's *The Moon and Sixpence* in 1957, then in 1966 came the historic *Moses und Aron*, and in 1970 Tippett's *The Knot Garden*. He had major successes at Glyndebourne with Cavalli's *La Calisto* in 1971 and *Il ritorno d'Ulisse in patria* a year later. In 1973 he produced *The Marriage of Figaro* at Glyndebourne that was both naturalistic and highly erotic – it was acclaimed as a masterpiece and reached a far wider public by being televised. On the hundredth anniversary of Wagner's death he produced the Ring Cycle at Bayreuth with Sir Georg Solti conducting. He was knighted in 1977 and published his diaries in 1983.

Hugo von Hofmannsthal (1874–1929)

Like Boito, fellow librettist von Hofmannsthal was also a man of many parts – in his case novelist, poet and playwright. He was writing from a young age but it was his meeting with Richard Strauss in 1900 that was to turn his pen to the service of opera, and he went on to write the libretti for *Elektra*, *Der Rosenkavalier*, *Ariadne auf Naxos*, *Die Aegyptische Helena*, *Arabella* and *Die Frau ohne Schatten*. In 1920, with Max Reinhardt, he established the Salzburg Festival and in 1925 wrote a screenplay for the film version of *Der Rosenkavalier*.

Herbert von Karajan (1908–1989)

Herbert von Karajan was the legendary conductor of the Berlin Philharmonic for thirty-five years and is the best-selling classical music recording artist ever. Born in Salzburg, Austria, he was a child prodigy as a pianist but his teachers at the Mozarteum in Salzburg and the Vienna School of Music and Performing Arts introduced him to conducting. In 1929 he made his professional debut as a conductor with *Salome* in Salzburg, and in 1933 he made his debut at the Salzburg Festival conducting the Walpurgisnacht Scene in *Faust*. The following year he conducted the Vienna Philharmonic and was soon conducting internationally in Paris, Stockholm, Brussels and Amsterdam. In 1937 he conducted *Fidelio* and *Tristan und Isolde* in Berlin. It was not, though, just German music that he favoured, his remarkably wide range including Italian *verismo*, a passionate and dramatic *Tosca*, a sublime *La Bohème* at La Scala with Zeffirelli and a fine *Otello*. In 1957, as well as being conductor for life of the Berlin Philharmonic, he became artistic director of the Vienna State Opera and the Salzburg Festival and he founded the Salzburg Easter Festival in 1967. In his later career he became increasingly interested in production and was often producer, lighting director and conductor all rolled into one. Von Karajan had an extraordinary ability to draw an exquisite and profound sound from both orchestra and singers and produce what one critic called 'clouds of ecstasy'. He has given many legendary interpretations – many of which have been recorded for posterity – and perhaps most lauded of all was *Tristan und Isolde* with the Berlin Philharmonic.

DID YOU KNOW?

Von Karajan was a key player in the development of the compact disc, appearing at the press conference announcing the new technology and conducting on the first ever digital recording – Mozart's *The Magic Flute*.

Rudolf Kempe (1910–1976)

Born in Dresden, Kempe studied piano, violin and oboe at the Orchestra School of the Dresden State Opera School and became an oboist and repetiteur in opera and orchestral music under Strauss, Klemperer and Furtwängler. He began conducting in Leipzig in 1934 but the outbreak of war led to a call-up and Kempe, rather than fighting, entertained the troops, conducting at the Chemnitz Opera House. After the war he became director of the Dresden Opera, moving in 1951 to the Vienna State Opera, conducting *The Magic Flute*, *Simon Boccanegra* and *Capriccio*. He conducted in Munich and at the Royal Opera House, Covent Garden where he was soon established as a favourite conductor of *Salome*, *Elektra*, *Der Rosenkavalier*, *Un Ballo in Maschera*, *Madama Butterfly* and Wagner's Ring Cycle. He continued to perform as a pianist but shunned the glare of publicity enjoyed by many performers and in later life was focused on teaching young musicians.

Otto Klemperer (1885–1973)

Born in Breslau (then in Germany though now in Poland), Klemperer studied at the Conservatory in Frankfurt and with Hans Pfitzner in Berlin. It was Mahler who recommended him to the Prague National Theatre and he went on to conduct in Hamburg and around Germany, culminating in Berlin in 1927 and breaking ground with new music including Janacek's *From the House of the Dead*, Arnold Schoenberg's *Erwartung* and Igor Stravinsky's *Oedipus Rex* and *Mavra*, as well as Puccini and Verdi. As a Jew, he was forced to leave Germany in 1933 when the Nazis came into power, and went to America where he was essentially a concert conductor. He returned to opera at Covent Garden with *Fidelio*, *The Magic Flute* and *Lohengrin*. His *Fidelio* was legendary for its emotional depth and intensity.

Charles Mackerras (1925–)

Born in New York State of Australian parents, Mackerras returned to Sydney when he was just two and later studied oboe, piano and composition at the New South Wales State Conservatorium of Music. He became principal oboist of the Sydney Symphony then relocated to London in 1946, winning a British Council scholarship to study conducting in Prague. In 1948 he returned and became a champion of Janacek, conducting *Katya Kavanova*, *The Makropoulos Case* and *From the House of the Dead* at Sadler's Wells Opera, later to become the English National Opera. His enormous repertoire included Mozart, Verdi, Wagner, Puccini and Arthur Sullivan. As well as being Musical Director of ENO, he conducted at Covent Garden, the Metropolitan in New York, Welsh National Opera and Sydney Opera House. He was knighted in 1979.

DID YOU KNOW?

Charles Mackerras was only the second person to be Honorary President of the Edinburgh Festival Society, the first being Yehudi Menuhin.

Gustav Mahler (1860–1911)

Mahler was an immensely successful composer – but not of operas. He wrote only two, very early in his career, neither ever published. He was nevertheless one of the greatest of all operatic conductors. After working in Prague and Hamburg, he rose in dizzying succession from conductor to director and to artistic director of the Vienna Opera in just one year, 1897, where he remained until 1907. During his time there he made the Vienna Opera the greatest in the world, spending a fortune but making it pay its way while building a superb company and producing and conducting Mozart, Wagner and Verdi. He conducted the first Ring Cycle at Covent Garden in 1892. In 1907 he went to the Met in New York, then became conductor of the New York Philharmonic Orchestra. Regarded as an artistic director, he often made enemies, was often the victim of anti-Semitic press attacks and his marriage, too, was difficult, with a much-publicized infidelity by his wife, Alma. He died of a blood infection at the age of fifty, leaving his last symphony unfinished.

> **DID YOU KNOW?**
> According to Alma, Mahler's widow – and notoriously unreliable
> biographer – Mahler's last word was 'Mozart' or 'dear little Mozart'.

Zubin Mehta (1936–)

Born in Bombay (now Mumbai) in India, Zubin Mehta is known as one of
the most fiery conductors in his interpretations of western music generally
and, particularly, in opera. He studied in Vienna, where he made his
conducting debut in 1958. After winning the International Conducting
Competition in Liverpool he became assistant conductor and soon chief
conductor of the Liverpool Philharmonic. His debut as an opera conductor
was in 1963 with *Tosca* in Montreal and from the sixties he was conducting
regularly at La Scala, Vienna, Salzburg, Covent Garden, Chicago, Florence
and the Met in New York. He was music director of the Bavarian State
Opera from 1998 to 2006. Some of his legendary performances include
Tristan und Isolde in Rome in 1972 and *Turandot*, first as a recording with
Joan Sutherland and later in a tour of the opera to Florence and Beijing (in
co-operation with the Chinese film director Zhang Yimou), where it was
staged (and filmed) in its original location, the Forbidden City, with over
300 extras and soldiers.

Jonathan Miller (1934–)

A true polymath, Jonathan Miller trained as a medical doctor, he has been
a humourist (notably in the sixties comedy revue *Beyond the Fringe* with
Peter Cook, Dudley Moore and Alan Bennett), author, television presenter
and theatre director. Despite not being able to read music, he started
directing operas in the seventies to great acclaim. His first productions
were for Kent Opera and Glyndebourne and he went on to English
National Opera in 1978 with *The Marriage of Figaro*, followed by a hugely
successful Mafia-style *Rigoletto* and a hilarious *Mikado* that featured the
comedian Eric Idle as Ko-Ko (with a very contemporary list of those who

'won't be missed') and set in a black and white art deco hotel. He directed Monteverdi's *Orfeo* in Manchester and Bristol and *Der Rosenkavalier* in Tokyo. After a prolonged break, he returned to ENO in 2009 with *La Bohème* and in 2010 Donizetti's *The Elixir of Love*, set in fifties small-town America. He was knighted in 2003.

Lorenzo da Ponte (1749–1838)

Born near Venice as Emanuele Conegliano, Lorenzo da Ponte took the name of the Bishop of Ceneda who officiated at his baptism and conversion from Judaism to Catholicism along with the rest of his family when he was fourteen years old. He intended to become a teacher and was ordained a Catholic priest but his life took a somewhat more unorthodox route when he took a married mistress, delivered their child and then set up a brothel. Banished from Venice, da Ponte set off for Austria, and took up the post of Emperor Joseph II's Poet of the Theatres. He wrote the libretti for operas by Antonio Salieri and, most importantly, for Mozart's *Marriage of Figaro*, *Don Giovanni* and *Così fan tutte*. These alone would have ensured his reputation, but after the death of the Emperor, da Ponte fell into debt and fled to America. Here he became the first professor of Italian literature at Columbia College and established Italian opera in the 1820s and 1830s in New York, starting with *Don Giovanni*.

Max Reinhardt (1873–1943)

Reinhardt was an Austrian director best known for his theatre productions rather than opera, but he introduced music and choreography to them in an entirely new way and made Berlin Europe's theatre capital. In 1911 he produced the first *Der Rosenkavalier* and Strauss dedicated *Ariadne auf Naxos* to him as thanks. In 1920, with Richard Strauss and Hugo von Hofmannsthal, he established the Salzburg Festival. After the Anschluss of Austria to Nazi Germany in 1938, he fled to England and then to the US. In America he became involved in directing for the theatre and films, including a notable *A Midsummer Night's Dream* with James Cagney and Mickey Rooney.

Georg Solti (1912–1997)

Born in Budapest to a Jewish family, Solti decided he wanted to become a conductor at the age of fourteen when he heard Erich Kleiber conduct Beethoven's Fifth Symphony. He studied at the Franz Liszt Academy and made his debut as a conductor in 1928 at the Budapest Opera with *The Marriage of Figaro*. It was on the same day that Hitler annexed Austria and Solti soon fled to Switzerland to escape anti-Semitism. He made his name in Munich after the war, and especially in Frankfurt, where he gave the German premiere of Berg's *Lulu*. In 1951 he made his debut at the Salzburg Festival conducting Mozart's *Idomeneo*. He became Music Director of Covent Garden in 1961 and stayed there for ten years. He gave some remarkable interpretations of Verdi, Strauss and Wagner there, some of his highlights being *Tristan und Isolde*, *Arabella*, *Elektra* and *Otello*. He conducted some remarkable Mozart there too, including *Don Giovanni* with Zeffirelli and a sensuous *Carmen*. In 1983 he conducted the Ring Cycle at Bayreuth and he has left a remarkable catalogue of recordings, including the Ring and the operas of Mozart, Strauss and Verdi, most of which have been remastered and re-released on CD. He was knighted in 1971.

Arturo Toscanini (1867–1957)

Regarded as one of the greatest conductors of the twentieth century, Toscanini was renowned for his intensity, his ferocious dedication to music, his remarkable musical memory – and his volcanic outbursts against singers, musicians and anyone who stood in the way of his vision. Born in Parma, Italy, he won a scholarship to the local conservatory. He was originally a cellist and played in the pit in the 1887 premiere of Verdi's *Otello*. He sprang to fame in Rio de Janeiro by taking over from a series of unsatisfactory conductors at the request of the musicians and singers and conducted *Aida* from memory to massive acclaim – at the age of nineteen. He conducted the premiere of Leoncavallo's *Pagliacci* in Milan in 1892 and *La Bohème* in 1896 and became chief conductor of La Scala in 1898, staying there for twenty years and conducting not only the Italian repertoire but Wagner, Strauss's *Salome* and Debussy's *Pelléas et Mélisande*. He was at the Met in New York from 1908 to 1915 where he premiered Puccini's *La fanciulla del west*. He returned to La Scala in 1921, ushering in one of the greatest periods in the theatre's history when he premiered Boito's *Nerone* and Puccini's *Turandot* and gave legendary performances of *Falstaff* and *Lucia di Lammermoor*. He was the first non-German conductor to appear at Bayreuth. In the thirties he conducted at the Salzburg Festival and at the inaugural concert in 1936 of the Palestine Symphony Orchestra, touring with them in Jerusalem, Cairo and Alexandria. He opposed fascism in Italy and its leader Benito Mussolini, and had his phone tapped, his passport confiscated and possibly was beaten up by the blackshirts for his pains. After an international outcry he was allowed to leave and did not return to Italy until 1946. In the US, the NBC Orchestra was created for him, and he made his first broadcast in 1937. Toscanini retired aged eighty-seven and died two years later.

DID YOU KNOW?
Toscanini had a tendency to hum while he was conducting and this can be clearly heard on some of his recordings, notably *La Bohème* and Verdi's *Requiem*.

Luciano Visconti (1906–1976)

Best known now as a film director, Visconti was just as famed as a director of theatre and opera. Born into a wealthy aristocratic family in Milan that had been connected with La Scala for centuries, it was no surprise that he was exposed to the arts from an early age. He was one of the first people to see Callas's extraordinary dramatic potential and he worked with her at La Scala on *La Vestale*, *La Sonnambula*, *La Traviata* and *Anna Bolena*. These productions made both Visconti's and Callas's names and were noted not only for their dramatic realism but the beauty and detail of the productions. Perhaps the most legendary of his productions was the 1958 Covent Garden *Don Carlos*. It was remarkable for its romantic realism and featured a distant, magical Chateau of Fontainebleau and a grey Monastery of San Giusto where monks and kneeling statues were almost indistinguishable until the monks started to come to life. With Bernstein he gave the Vienna State Opera one of the greatest productions of *Falstaff*.

Wieland Wagner (1917–1966)

The grandson of Richard Wagner, with his brother, Wolfgang, Wieland ran the Bayreuth Festival from 1951 until his death, when Wolfgang continued alone. He is credited with transforming the Bayreuth productions, abandoning naturalism in favour of symbolism and psychological insight. In the forefront of European drama as much as opera, the brothers started to use lighting to dramatic effect, plus minimalized sets and props, providing the most vivid and truthful understanding. He also staged Verdi, Beethoven, Bizet, Strauss, Orff, Gluck and Berg in Stuttgart, London, Paris and Brussels. Wolfgang continued producing until 2008 and was also a formidable talent. He made extensive renovations to the Bayreuth Festspielhaus and brought in a number of guest producers with sometimes controversial interpretations, such as Patrice Chéreau in 1976.

Franco Zeffirelli (1923–)

Like Visconti, Zeffirelli is best known to the general public as a film director, but his renown as a theatre and especially opera director is just as great. Born in Florence, he was only six when his mother died, and he was brought up under the eye of the British expatriate community, eventually resulting in the semi-autobiographical film *Tea with Mussolini*. He was greatly influenced by Visconti and he first became well known in the opera world by working with Visconti's favourite soprano, Callas, in *Il Turco in Italia*. But it was with Joan Sutherland in *Lucia di Lammermoor* at Covent Garden in 1959 that he became internationally famous. It was soon clear – in *Cavalleria Rusticana* and *Pagliacci* in 1959 at Covent Garden – that Zeffirelli had a genius for getting singers to act in a new, naturalistic way. *Falstaff*, *Don Giovanni* and *L'Elisir d'Amore* all followed in the UK, but it was his *Tosca* with Maria Callas and Tito Gobbi at Covent Garden in 1964 that has been hailed as the ultimate interpretation of the opera. Act II was filmed. Zeffirelli went on to combine his love of film and opera in a series of films, including *Cavalleria Rusticana* and *Pagliacci* with Plácido Domingo, *La Traviata* with Domingo and Teresa Stratas, *Otello* with Domingo and Katia Ricciarelli and *Don Carlo* with Pavarotti and Daniela Dessi. He was awarded an honorary knighthood in 2004.